Shadow Warriors
Of The 21st Century

SAS

Shadow Warriors
Of The 21st Century

Barry Davies

LEWIS
INTERNATIONAL, INC.

First published in the United States in 2002 by
Lewis International, Inc.
Copyright © 2002 The Brown Reference Group plc

Lewis International, Inc.
2201 N.W. 102 Place, #1
Miami, F1 33172 USA

Tel: 305-436-7984 / 800-259-5962
Fax: 305-436-7985 / 800-664-5095

ISBN 1-930983-15-8

Editorial and Design:
The Brown Reference Group plc
8 Chapel Place
Rivington Street
London
EC2A 3DQ
UK
www.brownreference.com

Printed in Hong Kong

Editors: Peter Darman, Chris McNab
Picture Research: Barry Davies
Design: The Brown Reference Group plc
Production: Alastair Gourlay

PICTURE CREDITS
Corbis/Holland Davies: 179
Corbis/Sygma: 186 (both)
Barry Davies: 10, 11, 12, 16, 18, 19, 20, 24, 26, 27, 28-29, 30 (both),
31, 32, 33, 34, 35 (both), 36, 37, 38, 39 (both), 40 (both), 41, 42, 43,
44, 45, 46, 47, 48, 48-49, 50-51, 52, 53 (bottom), 54, 55, 56 (both), 57,
58, 59 (both), 60, 61, 62 (both), 63, 64, 65, 66 (both), 67, 68, 69, 70-
71, 73, 76, 77, 78, 79, 80-81, 82, 84, 85, 86, 87, 100, 101, 108-109, 110,
111, 112, 113, 114, 115, 116, 119 (both), 120, 122-123, 124, 125, 126-
127, 128-129, 130, 131, 132, 133, 135, 136-137, 138, 139 (both), 140,
141, 143, 144, 146, 147 (both), 148, 148-149, 150, 151, 152, 152-153,
153, 154, 154-155, 156, 156-157, 157, 158, 159, 160, 161, 162-163, 166
(both), 167, 168, 169, 170, 171, 172, 173, 174, 176-177, 178
FN Herstal: 75, 103 (top), 107, 145
Heckler & Koch: 105 (both), 142 (top)
PA Photos: 22, 23, 95
Popperfoto: 8-9, 13, 14, 17, 88-89, 90, 92-93, 94, 98
Private collection: 74, 83, 99, 102, 103 (bottom)
Rex Features: 53 (top), 97, 183, 185, 189
SIG Sauer: 142 (bottom)
US Government: 164-165, 180, 180-181

Contents

Introduction

This book is an analysis of how the Anti-Terrorist Team of the British Special Air Service (SAS) fights modern-day terrorism, a scourge that spreads death and disorder across the globe. The *Al Qaeda* attacks of 11 September 2001 against the twin towers of the World Trade Center in New York are the most recent examples of international terrorist outrages. Terrorists can strike anywhere at any time. They spread fear and insecurity wherever they strike, and they operate with apparent total impunity. However, the forces of law and democracy have powerful weapons in their armouries to combat the forces of terrorism. Chief among them is the SAS.

The Counter-Revolutionary Warfare (CRW) cell was set up within the SAS structure in the 1960s when the Regiment recognized the growing terrorist threat. CRW teams soon perfected early techniques in VIP protection, surveillance and anti-terrorist tactics. They were first put into use in May 1972 when an anonymous phone call was received at the offices of Cunard in London saying that six bombs had been planted on the liner *Queen Elizabeth II*. These would be detonated unless a ransom was paid. A team of SAS and Special Boat Service (SBS) men were parachuted into the Atlantic from a C-130 transport aircraft in order to carry out a full search of the ship. As it turned out the whole thing was a hoax. However, a few months later, at the 1972 Munich Olympics, 11 Israeli athletes were murdered by Palestinian terrorists. The governments of the West had no option but to form dedicated counter-terrorist and hostage-rescue units.

In Britain counter-terrorism missions became the responsibility of the SAS. For the first time a dedicated team of highly trained men would stand ready to combat terrorism. Today, the SAS Anti-Terrorist Team is equipped with state-of-the-art weaponry and devices which allows it to assault any form of terrorist stronghold. These "shadow warriors" are an élite within an élite. This book is dedicated to these anonymous heroes who are in the frontline of the fight against international terror.

Barry Davies, Spain 2002

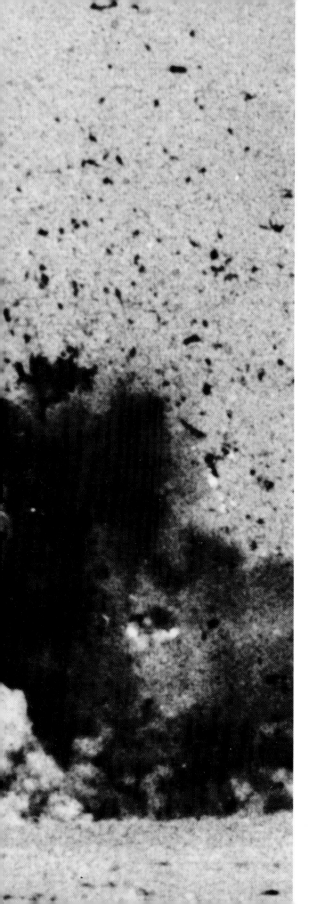

CHAPTER 1

The Birth of Modern Terrorism

The Special Air Service became involved in anti-terrorism as a result of the terrorist outrages around the world in the 1960s. Western governments were at first defenceless against international terrorist groups, but by the end of the decade were fighting back.

Terrorism and guerrilla warfare have been with us since long before the birth of Christ. However, it is fair to say that terrorism in the modern meaning of the word started in the late 1940s and by the late 1960s, an age of revolution, it was in full swing.

What do we mean by terrorism? Its motives can cover a wide spectrum, and can include nationalists fighting for a homeland, religious fundamentalists or political groups pushing for social change. Though usually left-wing or revolutionary in intent, terrorists can also act from a right-wing position.

In America and Western Europe during the 1960s and 1970s there was a wave of antipathy against the "Bomb" and the Vietnam War. It was a period when the Establishment was made to feel very unstable and insecure. Organizations such as the Palestine Liberation Organization (PLO), Baader-Meinhof Group and, at the end of the decade, the Irish Republican Army (IRA) were at the sharp end of this rebellion. It was an age when individual freedom

Left: *In the full glare of the world's media, the Popular Front for the Liberation of Palestine blows up the hijacked airliners on Dawson's Field in September 1970.*

Above: Yasser Arafat, the founder of Al-Fatah *who later became leader of the PLO, a position he holds to this day.*

funding and equipping its soldiery known as *Al-Fatah*. Yasser Arafat was elected overall leader in 1969. The problem for the PLO was one of Arab disunity. As each state constantly bickered with its neighbour, fringe and rival groups within the PLO received separate sponsorship. On the one hand Egypt would back George Habash's Popular Front for the Liberation of Palestine (PFLP). The PFLP was set up in 1967, and though Palestinian was also a Marxist group and as such had much in common with other Marxist groups worldwide. On the other hand, Syria supported the Ahmad Jibril group, which had split from the PFLP in 1968. At times they were friends, and at times they were fighting each other.

Middle Eastern terrorist groupings are complex, but at this point it would be useful to have some insight into the various personalities and organizations that contributed towards this new breed of terrorism.

was thought of as being more important than the organized authority it challenged.

Ironically, during the Cold War between the Warsaw Pact countries and the states of the North Atlantic Treaty Organisation (NATO) many foreign governments saw terrorist organizations as irregular soldiers. They supplied funding, weapons and training, using the organizations to further their own ends. Yet while some terrorist groups truly believed their cause was just, others were simply anti-Establishment. Three groups in particular emphasize the diversity in terrorist aims: the PLO, the Baader-Meinhof Group and the IRA.

In 1964 President Nasser of Egypt helped set up the PLO and from a shaky start it was to become the main voice of the Palestinian people, which it remains to this day. It sought to establish a Palestinian state on land occupied by Israel, and in October 1974 was recognized by Arab states to be the sole representative of the Palestinian people. Most Arab nations backed the organization,

What Makes a Terrorist?

People do not just become terrorists or hijackers – there is always an axis on which all events turn. In the PLO's case it was the foundation of Israel in 1948. As the British left Palestine in the same year, a bitter internal war started. Many Palestinian families were forced to flee their homeland. At the height of the initial fighting, the Israelis drove out many non-Jewish families, often at the point of a gun. Hundreds were killed in the fighting that erupted. Subsequently forced to live in refugee camps in conditions of daily survival, many burned with the desire to return to Palestine. Among these thousands of refugees were two young men: George Habash and Wadi Haddad.

George Habash was the son of a wealthy grain merchant, born in Lydda in Palestine in 1925, whose family were practising Christians. Towards the end of the 1940s Habash, like so many young hopefuls in the region, was attending class at the

American University in Beirut. He was training to be a doctor of medicine, and was an intelligent man working hard at his studies. In May 1948, aged 23, he was nearly ready to leave the university and continue his dream to start up a clinic on his own. However, in that same month the British Army withdrew from Palestine, and almost immediately the fighting started. Within months his family were driven into exile.

Wadi Haddad, the son of a teacher, was born in Safad in Galilee just before World War II. But by the age of nine he too had become a refugee, and was forced with his family to lead a peripatetic life. The difference between the two men lay in their intellects: Habash was a brilliant student, whereas Haddad had struggled academically and qualified as a doctor with difficulty. By profession both were committed to the preservation of life, but the trauma of their upbringing embittered them.

Below: *George Habash, the head of the PFLP and the brains behind terrorism and hijacking in the 1970s.*

For Habash and Haddad, the mid-1960s was a decade when revolutionary rhetoric was in plentiful supply throughout the world. This was an era of extremes and dreams. Terrorism, death and disruption at one end of the scale, and hippies, flower-power, peace and freedom of speech at the other. In the melting pot of the Middle East, Habash and Haddad dreamed of rebellion. Both were educated, middle-class men who had been displaced from the land of their birth. In the years to follow Habash became so embittered that he discarded his religious beliefs and replaced them with Marxist concepts. His medical equipment was exchanged for an arsenal of guns, and from his intellect he created the PFLP. It seems ironic that a man who had professed to be Christian was to become the leader of the most extreme Palestinian terrorist organization ever known.

After members of the PFLP had fire-bombed a Marks & Spencer's store in London on 18 July 1969, Habash is quoted as having said: "When we set fire to a store in London, those few flames are worth the burning down of two kibbutz [in Israel]." Although he made these provocative statements, Habash was actually less of an extremist than Wadi Haddad.

The Terrorists go to War

During the late 1960s there was growing coordination between various revolutionary groups, and while Western governments recognized this they chose to ignore it. George Habash had been instrumental in setting up these guerrilla liaisons. Dedicated training camps were to be the ground for the conception and birth of transnational terrorism. Here, the fighters were trained in the use of small arms, such as Soviet Kalashnikovs, and taught the tactics of terrorism and guerrilla warfare. It was at the camp north of Amman, for example, that the entire Baader-Meinhof Group was trained. At this time, strong

bonds were formed at these camps between the Palestinian groups and European terrorist bodies. Haddad went on to form his own PFLP Special Operations Group, and maintained contacts with a number of international terrorist groups, including the Italian Red Brigades. In particular, Haddad got on very well with members of the Baader-Meinhof Group, and they were to become very important to him. He was responsible for such dramatic acts as the multiple hijacking of three aircraft to Dawson's Field in Jordan in September 1970 (see below). That affair in turn led to the "Black September" expulsion of the Palestinians from Jordan, and to the massacre of 26 people by the Japanese Red Army at Lod airport in Israel.

The first of the Palestinian hijacks occurred during the summer of 1968, when an Israeli El Al Boeing 707 flying from Rome to Tel Aviv was hijacked and diverted to Algiers. The Israeli passengers and crew were subsequently

Above: Dawson's Field may have been a triumph for the PFLP in terms of media exposure, but it gave King Hussein of Jordan the excuse he needed to turn on the Palestinians in his country.

imprisoned for two months. In December of that year, another El Al Boeing 707 was attacked. As the plane took off from Athens airport, the sound of grenades and submachine-gun fire was heard by the passengers. One of the passengers was killed, but the attackers were arrested. The European general public believed that the Israeli security forces did not have an adequate response to the export of Palestinian terrorism from the Middle East to Europe. Goaded into action, on 28 December at 09:15 hours Israeli special forces were landed by helicopter at the International Airport just south of the Lebanese capital, Beirut. Undeterred by a gun battle with Lebanese troops, the Israelis blew up 13 empty civilian aircraft belonging to the Lebanese Middle East Airlines and other Arab countries. The world was shocked by the audacity of the move, and condemned Israel as engaging in what is referred to as "state terrorism".

In February 1969, another El Al Boeing 707 was machine-gunned when it was preparing to take off from Zurich for Tel Aviv. The co-pilot was killed and five of the passengers were wounded. One of the attackers was killed on the plane by an Israeli guard. The surviving three terrorists were captured and sentenced to prison, but were later released when the PFLP carried out further hijacks. By now, airline passengers were becoming nervous and avoiding flights wherever possible. In August 1969 the PFLP, led by an armed female terrorist, again hijacked a plane, this time a TWA flight from Rome to Tel Aviv. The plane was taken to Damascus, where all the 213 passengers were released except for two Israelis. These men were held under threat of execution until they were exchanged for two

Below: Dawson's Field showed that the governments of Western Europe desperately needed specially trained anti-terrorist units to fight international terrorism.

Syrian pilots. The pilot's cabin was then rigged with explosives and the plane was destroyed. All the passengers spent the night at Damascus University. The sequence of hijacks was to culminate in a mass hijacking on 12 September 1970, when three Western aircraft were hijacked and flown to a desert airfield in Jordan known as Dawson's Field.

To understand the Dawson's Field story we have to trace the friendship of Wadi Haddad with an important member of his guerrilla squads, Leila Khaled. Leila Khaled was a close confidante of Wadi Haddad. Leila Khaled was an attractive, dark-haired, intelligent girl in her twenties. Her charisma and her successes had turned the young woman into a folk legend, and the Palestinians and Arab youth alike idolized her. She had been a teacher in Kuwait and, like Habash and Haddad before her, had studied at the American University in Beirut. She was just four years old when her family had been driven out of Palestine.

Khaled was at his house in July 1970 when it was attacked by Mossad (the Israeli Secret Service),

during one of its many attempts to kill him. On this occasion Khaled was discussing operational plans in the living room of Haddad's house. Suddenly there were several massive explosions, most of which seemed to hit the bedroom section of the building. Khaled and Wadi were both uninjured, and after the initial shock they ran to what was left of the bedroom. Here Wadi Haddad found his wife and eight-year-old son, both badly burned and disfigured. Mossad agents had just carried out a rocket attack on Haddad's home. They would soon strike back at the Israelis.

Khaled was to be part of a group that hijacked an Israeli Boeing 707 en route to New York, flying from Tel Aviv via Amsterdam. The original plan

Below: One of the West German helicopters that was riddled with bullets during the abortive rescue attempt to free Israeli hostages taken at the 1972 Munich Olympics.

appears to have been to send at least five terrorists to hijack the El Al aircraft. Haddad had chosen Khaled as she had become a most accomplished hijacker and was keen to tackle the heavily guarded Israeli airliner. He gave her the only copy of the navigation plans for the plane's destination. All five terrorists were to meet at Amsterdam airport (no one knew whether they had met before). Fortunately, at Amsterdam the suspicions of airport staff were alerted when three of the would-be hijackers tried to insist that their first-class seats should be located near the front of the plane, just by the pilot's cabin. The wary airport staff refused them passage and turned them away, barring their entry onto the plane. The uneasy terrorists failed to tell the other two operatives, who were in another passenger lounge waiting to embark, that they would not be on the plane. As the final call for all passengers was made over the airport public

address system, Leila Khaled and her co-conspirator made their way unknowingly to the aircraft. Khaled and her male companion sat together on the plane, but did not speak or appear to recognize one another. Although they must have realized that they were now on their own, they were determined to carry on with the hijack. Ten minutes after taking off, as they flew over the North Sea while the passengers were finishing their first drinks of the journey and beginning to relax, Khaled and Patrick Arguello leapt from their seats. Khaled waved her hands in the air, exposing the two grenades that she held. Her companion gestured towards the frightened passengers with a revolver. They shouted and threatened the 145 passengers and air stewards. As Arguello made his way towards the captain's cabin, he ordered an air stewardess to open the cabin door. However, he was intercepted and shot by a male steward (a sky marshal) who was carrying a gun, though not before the terrorist had also shot him.

Terror at 35,000ft

As Leila Khaled made her way into the first-class lounge, an unidentified young man, possibly a security guard, disarmed her. He grabbed her by the elbows and pushed her to the floor, then tied her hands and feet together with string and a man's neck tie. The plan had failed due to the courage of the crew and the captain of the Israeli plane. The pilot radioed a request for an emergency landing at Heathrow Airport. A full-scale police alert went into operation. As the plane flew over England, the male terrorist, Arguello, was kept out of sight of the passengers and died shortly before the plane touched down at Heathrow. The steward who had attempted to restrain him had been shot three times in the stomach, but went on to make a full recovery in hospital in England.

On 6 September 1970, an American TWA Boeing 707 carrying 145 passengers and 10 crew members was flying from Frankfurt to New York. During its flight over the French coastline the plane was hijacked and forced to fly to the Middle East, where the pilot was told to land at a desert airstrip in Jordan called Dawson's Field. The airfield had come under the control of the PFLP's guerrilla army and the hijack was part of its master plan. Dawson's Field is a dried-out strip of marshland 72km (45 miles) northeast of Amman. It had been originally used by the British in 1947 by Air Chief Marshal Sir Walter Dawson, hence its name. Next, a Swissair DC8 airliner flying from Zurich to New York with 140 passengers and 12 crew members on board was hijacked over central France. Once again the aircraft was redirected to the desert strip at Dawson's Field.

The Flight to Dawson's Field

The strip was in a very poor condition and the landings were risky: the chances of a serious crash landing were very high. The pilot cautiously attempted a full-flap landing and the aircraft jolted and pitched on the rough surface. The passengers closed their eyes tightly as they rushed towards the end of the strip, the plane shaking and juddering as the pilot applied maximum braking power. Then, a Pan American 747, again flying to New York and starting its journey from Amsterdam, was commandeered by the PFLP. This plane was hijacked by the remaining three terrorists who had failed in their attempt to go with Leila Khaled and her comrade. Again the three terrorists blundered, though. They could not force the pilot to take the aircraft to Dawson's Field because they did not have the ability to navigate it to this remote area; the navigation was to have been Leila's job. They therefore ordered the pilot to fly to Beirut where he was allowed to refuel.

The next day the plane with its 170 occupants flew to Cairo. Before they landed, though, the

Above: *The charred remains of one of the helicopters at Fürstenfeldbruck airport after a Black September terrorist had thrown a grenade into its fuselage.*

unpredictable attitude of the hijackers was brought home to the crew as they made the captain circle at low altitude several times so that they could spot familiar places from the air. The plane banked steeply as it started its final descent and the passengers, who by now were very anxious, gripped their seats in fear. The aircraft landed at the airport whereupon the passengers, crew and terrorists abandoned it. Before the hijackers left, on the orders of Haddad, they had wired the plane with incendiary grenades and explosives, primed to go off just as they all cleared the plane. The subsequent explosion blew it to bits.

Meanwhile, at Dawson's Field the PFLP held over 300 hostages, consisting of crew and passengers. Without a ground power unit the discomfort inside the hijacked aircraft reached appalling levels. During the day the heat was intense while at night it was freezing cold. With complete impunity the guerrillas had rigged the planes with booby traps and explosives, and although the Jordanian Army sent in 14 helicopters full of heavily armed troops, they were of little use. They could do little more than surround Dawson's Field – they did not want to provoke the PFLP guerrillas taking action against their hostages.

The PFLP made it clear that it would not free the hostages or aircraft until Khaled and six other imprisoned Palestinians were released. Three of the Palestinians were held in Germany and three were held in Swiss jails. The three held in Switzerland were serving 12-year sentences as a result of an earlier, abortive hijack on a 707 aircraft in 1969 at Zurich airport. So, in temperatures of over 38 degrees centigrade (100 degrees fahrenheit) during the day and bitingly cold nights the passengers had to sit and wait, suffering in silence. Back in Great Britain, Edward Heath, the newly elected British prime minister, was in a quandary over the treatment of Khaled. As the Heath Government struggled for an answer, the PFLP reinforced the administration's anxiety by blowing up all three planes at Dawson's Field in front of the world's media. The 300 hostages were taken by the guerrillas and the Red Cross to hotels and houses situated between Amman and north Jordan. The hostages came from many different countries, so diplomatic relations were stretched in every direction. The countries involved were the USA,

Below: The bloody aftermath of the botched rescue attempt at Fürstenfeldbruck. This incident led European states to create dedicated anti-terrorist units.

Israel, West Germany, Switzerland and Great Britain, and representatives of all these states met in Washington to discuss their options. The Swiss quickly capitulated to the hijackers' demands. As they did so the hijackers gave Great Britain an ultimatum that Leila Khaled was to be freed by Thursday 10 September, 03:00 hours British time, or the British hostages would be shot. When the hijackers blew up the aircraft, Edward Heath decided that the safest course for the British hostages was to release Khaled.

Khaled was taken from West Drayton police station and moved to Ealing police station, which had been specifically turned into a virtual four-storey fortress. There were armed policemen at every entrance (the fear was not of her escaping but of someone trying to get in). A day or two later, she was taken from Ealing police station to board an RAF plane that flew her to Beirut. En route to Beirut the plane stopped in Switzerland and West Germany to pick up the six other terrorists who

Above: The Baader-Meinhoff Group were terrorists without a real cause. Andreas Baader (top), Carl Raspe (bottom left) and Ulrike Meinhof (bottom right) were students who planned to bring down the West German Government by violence.

were part of the deal. The terrorists had achieved everything that they had requested. Due to the exploits of the PFLP, hijacking subsequently became a useful terrorist weapon. After all, if it had worked at Dawson's Field then it could work elsewhere for other terrorist groups.

At this time terrorist groups around the world seem to have held the upper hand, and in many cases a loose alliance was beginning to form between the various organizations. For example, when the *Sekigun-ha* (Japanese Red Army) staged a machine-gun massacre at Israel's Lod Airport in May 1972 (25 people were killed and a further 76 injured), it was acting on behalf of the Palestinians.

In return the Palestinians offered the *Sekigun-ha* training facilities, as well as logistical support. Nevertheless, it was the emergence of a Palestinian group known as Black September that was to make the biggest impression. As far back as 1968, groups of Palestinian *Fatah* had attacked the Israelis. They blew up buses and threw bombs indiscriminately, killing, maiming and generally terrorizing the population of Israel. The Israelis hit back hard, but despite several attempts failed to locate the leaders of the various groups, many of whom had escaped to Jordan where King Hussein offered them accommodation and a base from which to fight. It was a bad move for the Jordanian monarch. Soon, the Palestinian presence became a major force in the land, making themselves unpopular with their hosts. The *Fatah* took no notice of Jordanian requests to halt its attacks against Israel, to the point where the king himself came under pressure from his own army to take action.

Black September

With his authority threatened, King Hussein at last agreed to send his Bedouin fighters to control the Palestinians. It was a bloodbath. During the month of September 1970, over 2000 Palestinians died at the hands of their Arab brothers. So brutal was the fighting that many Palestinians fled to the borders of Israel, seeking asylum and imprisonment rather than face the wrath of the Jordanians (the PLO had been expelled from Jordan altogether by July 1971).

Amidst these events "Black September" was born. Its aim was to act independently as a secret branch of the PLO, organized by Arafat to take revenge against Jordan. On 28 November 1971, Prime Minister Wasfi Tell, a man very close to King Hussein and opposed to *Fatah*, was publicly assassinated. He was gunned down in the entrance to the Cairo Sheraton while attending the Arab Defence League Council. As he lay dying, a terrorist lapped at his blood. Three weeks later the Jordanian Ambassador to Great Britain was shot in London, but survived. Then the Jordanian Airlines office in Rome was bombed, with similar attacks following in Hamburg, Rotterdam and Bonn. When an airliner was blown up in mid-air, Black September was ensuring it dominated world news. The organization's leader, Ali Hassan, masterminded these acts, giving him the nickname the Red Prince. Pleased with its success against Jordan, Black September quickly turned its guns against Israel. Modelling itself on George Habash's PFLP, Black September terrorists hijacked a Sabena aircraft in May 1972 and ordered it to land at Lod. The plan misfired, though, and two of the terrorists were killed and two more captured. Ali Hassan went back to the drawing board. In September 1972, the perfect terrorist opportunity arrived when the West Germans won the right to stage the Olympic Games in Munich. As a direct result of Germany's conscience over the Holocaust, and the Nazi Olympic Games held in 1936, the government bent over backwards to please and accommodate the Israeli athletic team. Even when Yasser Arafat applied to put forward a Palestinian team, the West German Olympic Committee totally ignored his request. That the games coincided with the second anniversary of "Black September" encouraged Ali Hassan to carry out his most daring plan yet.

Terror at the Olympics

The Olympic village had been deliberately planned with the minimum of security, reducing the unpleasant memories of Germany's Nazi past. The Israeli team was billeted in Connollystrasse 31, separated from the public by a wire fence and the occasional patrolling guard.

A little before 04:30 hours on the morning of 5 September, a group of young men were seen climbing the fence. This was was not an uncommon

sight, as many of the athletes stayed out late in the beer halls of Munich. But these were no athletes, they were Black September terrorists intent on killing Israelis or bartering their lives for the release of jailed Palestinians. Bursting into the Israeli accommodation, the seven terrorists opened fire, killing many athletes and capturing nine for hostages. The Israeli Government, true to its firm policy, refused to cave in and free any prisoners.

Above: Hans Martin Schleyer. A captain of German industry, he was kidnapped a month before the Mogadishu hijack in October 1977. His fate was sealed when GSG 9 made a successful assault on the aircraft; he was found dead a few days later.

West Germany refused the offer of Israeli troops to counter the problem, and decided to attempt a rescue plan of its own. By 22:00 hours that same day, a grey army bus transferred both terrorists and hostages to the edge of the Olympic village, where they climbed into two helicopters requested by the

terrorists for evacuation. They flew to Fürstenfeldbruck, some 24km (15 miles) to the west, where they landed in a well-illuminated area. A requested Lufthansa 727 aircraft sat on the tarmac a little over 91m (300ft) away, and two of the terrorists left the helicopter to check it out.

At 22:44 hours German police snipers, lying in wait to ambush the terrorists, opened fire. A fierce firefight ensued. The bolt-action rifles of the German police were no match for the automatic fire of the terrorists' AK-47s. Israeli diplomats watched helplessly from the control tower of Fürstenfeldbruck air base as inexperienced and ill-equipped German sharpshooters failed to kill all the terrorists in the first volley. Three were still alive, and they fired their guns and detonated their grenades to kill the handcuffed hostages, who were slaughtered as they sat in the helicopters. In the end, the three terrorists were overpowered and captured, but not before they had killed all nine hostages. A police sergeant who stepped out from the control tower also took a bullet through the head. Waves of shock reverberated around the world, with the massacre seen as both a human tragedy and a warning that international terrorism had to be fought.

The "Wrath of God"

In reprisal, the Israelis organized hit squads nick-named the "Wrath of God". These teams were sent out to track down and eliminate all those who had taken part in the planning, preparation and participation in the Munich attack. They got almost all of them except the brains behind the whole operation: major international Palestinian playboy

Left: *The Establishment under attack. The bodyguard of Italian Christian Democrat leader Aldo Moro lies dead on the pavement following Moro's kidnapping by Red Brigade terrorists in March 1978. Moro was later murdered by his captors.*

Ali Hassan, the Red Prince. In 1995 I had reason to visit Norway while investigating a terrorist incident. The Israelis had tracked down Ali Hassan to a little town called Lillehammer in central Norway. The hit team sent in to kill him assassinated the wrong man. They murdered instead a Moroccan named Ahmed Bouchiki, who was totally innocent. He was shot dead in full view of his pregnant Norwegian wife. I spent several hours with the lady, who has now reverted back to her maiden name Torill Larsen. Her story was incredible: how one of the most sophisticated security agencies in the world could have mistaken her husband for a major international terrorist such as the Red Prince is a mystery. Meanwhile, the real Ali Hassan was under heavy security in Beirut, where he had just married a former Miss World beauty queen.

On the afternoon of 22 January 1979, Ali Hassan left his new wife, now six months pregnant, and set off in his distinctive "Chevy", sitting in the back squashed between two bodyguards. Several more "heavies" accompanied him in an escorting white Land Rover. His car moved slowly down Verdun Street and turned into Madame Curie Street. Someone had badly parked a white Volkswagen, making the street much narrower. As the Chevy negotiated past the Volkswagen, which had been packed with explosives, it detonated. Finally Mossad had got their man. Ali Hassan's body, together with those of his bodyguards, was blown to bits (unfortunately several other innocent tourists died in the explosion, including an English nurse). As it turned out, the woman who triggered the bomb was also British. Yasser Arafat helped carry Ali Hassan's coffin. Months later, on 15 May 1979, his former beauty queen widow gave birth to a son (whose arrival coincided with the anniversary of the creation of the state of Israel). She called him Ali Hassan Salameh.

The Israelis had achieved a victory, but there were many other Palestinian terrorists to fill Hassan's shoes, while in Western Europe there were revolutionary groups ready to challenge state power. In West Germany, for example, the popularity of Marxism among the student movement, coupled with widespread dissatisfaction with the domestic political and social situation, led to the creation of terrorist groups.

Baader-Meinhof (Red Army Faction)

In West Germany during the late 1960s and the mid-1970s, the Baader-Meinhof Group was waging its own terrorist war. The gang was named after its founders, Andreas Baader and Ulrike Meinhof. The Baader-Meinhof Group never seemed to have any justifiable cause for its terrorist activities aside from its general dislike of capitalism. It was comprised of a group of misguided young people who had let their powers of communication and intellect go beyond normal left-wing student activities. The Baader-Meinhof were no ordinary terrorists, though. The members operated on a basis of pure destructiveness – terrorism for terrorism's own sake. One of its slogans was: "Don't argue, destroy." The Baader-Meinhof Group eventually changed its name to the Red Army Faction in the late 1970s, a move that was supposed to align itself with international world terrorist organizations such as the Japanese Red Army. During this period of change Gudrun Ensslin, a female student who became the real female leader of Baader-Meinhof, formed an intense relationship with Andreas Baader and was much more involved with him than Ulrike Meinhof.

One day in Frankfurt the police were given a tip-off. It came from a man who thought that a garage

Below: The remains of the British Army truck that caught the full force of an Irish Republican Army (IRA) terrorist bomb at Warrenpoint, County Down, in 1979. The IRA was the SAS's most tenacious foe during the "troubles" in Ulster.

Above: *The funeral of Private Gary Ivan Barnes, the Parachute Regiment, who was killed during the IRA attack at Warrenpoint. Preventing such outrages became one of the SAS's counter-terrorist tasks during its operations in Northern Ireland.*

near him was being used to make bombs. The police started to watch the garage. On 1 June 1972, three men arrived at the garage. They were Andreas Baader and two other terrorists, Holger Meins and Jan-Carl Raspe. When the police approached the garage they were spotted by Raspe, who fired his gun at them and ran off, but was later detained. When the other two looked out from the garage doors to see what was going on, they saw the police coming towards them. Gesturing with his submachine gun, one of the officers ordered Baader and Meins back into the garage. As they complied another policeman drove his Audi car against the

garage doors to secure them. Baader started to fire at the doors but his shots were blind and no one was hit. So they remained trapped until police reinforcements arrived and the garage was totally surrounded by 150 officers, all pointing guns at the besieged men.

Despite the futility of the situation, Baader and Meins refused to surrender. They continued to smoke cigarettes and wave their guns at the police through the window. About an hour later the police decided to throw containers of tear gas into the garage, through holes in the rear of the building. Thinking that this would finish the siege, the police announced through loud speakers that the terrorists should throw out their guns and surrender. Slowly the two pushed on one of the garage doors, which was still trapped by the Audi. Eventually the police shifted the car, whereupon

Above: During the 1970s the SAS was involved in a number of incidents involving potential terrorist threats. Here, SAS soldiers parachute into the Atlantic in May 1972 to investigate suspicious objects aboard the liner Queen Elizabeth II.

the door opened wider and Baader threw out the tear gas canisters, laughing as he did so and forcing all the police to back off. At 19:45 hours the police sent for an armoured car with four officers in it. The operation was becoming farcical: all this armed police presence against two men in a garage. Finally the two men were given one last chance to

surrender. They refused. The police then stormed the front of the garage using the armoured vehicle as a battering ram. At the same time they threw more tear gas cylinders at the garage. The armoured vehicle was not able to get through the garage doors, though. In fact it just forced them shut more tightly, and this meant that the tear gas containers did not go into the garage but went off where the police were located, forcing them to move back themselves. At the same time, Baader and Meins continued to fire their weapons from inside the garage. While all this chaos was going on, a policeman had gone into the building opposite the garage and entered a flat on the third floor. It gave an excellent view of the garage and the surrounding yard. Armed with a rifle with a telescopic sight, he watched the situation and recognized Andreas Baader. Taking up a position he took aim and fired at Baader, hitting him in the thigh. Baader fell screaming to the ground in agony. Again the two men were told to throw out their guns and surrender. Holger Meins complied and came out with his hands up. Baader lay where he had fallen, writhing and screaming on the floor of the garage as two police officers dressed in bullet-proof jackets then approached him. One of the police officers kicked the gun out of Baader's hand and they dragged him outside. Still ranting and raving, he was taken into an ambulance under heavy escort.

Tracking Down the Terrorists

The police now had several of the most wanted members of the gang in custody. During the previous 15 days the police had managed to apprehend Meinhof, Ensslin and Brigitte Monhaupt, all vital members of the group. All the prisoners were confined to isolation cells in separate prisons. On 5 October 1974, nearly two and a half years after their arrests, all five were indicted for five murders and taken to Stammhein high-security prison. The West German authorities appeared to have triumphed.

However, this was not the end of the Red Army Faction. On 30 July 1977, Dr Juergen Ponto, head of the Dresdner Bank, the second largest bank in Germany, was shot dead. The terrorists bluffed their way into his heavily guarded home and shot him in the head. His memorial service was well attended; most of those present represented the heads of industry and commerce. Among them was Hans Martin Schleyer. Schleyer was a director of Mercedes Benz and an important figure in German industry. At the service Schleyer is reported to have said: "The next victim of terrorism is almost certainly standing in this room now." As prophecies go he was spot on. He was predicting his own future.

In Great Britain, meanwhile, terrorist activity would suck the Special Air Service Regiment into an anti-terrorist role.

The Irish Republican Army (IRA)

Northern Ireland erupted into violence in the late 1960s, committing the British Army to the Province where it remains to this day. Operational cells of the Irish Republican Army (IRA), known as "active service units", carried out bombings, mortar attacks and assassinations against the security services. It was quick to learn the benefits of prestige targets, both in Northern Ireland and on the British mainland. In March 1979, for example, an IRA car bomb, planted in the House of Commons car park, killed Airey Neave, one of Prime Minister Margaret Thatcher's closest political and personal friends. On 27 August of the same year, the IRA assassinated Earl Mountbatten of Burma, the Queen's cousin, while on holiday in Ireland aboard his boat. Later that same day, an IRA bomb killed 18 soldiers at Warrenpoint, County Down.

The soldiers, from the 2nd Battalion, Parachute Regiment, were travelling in a four-ton truck along a road on the north shore of Carlingford Lough, close to the village of Warrenpoint. The lough at this point is so narrow that the south side, in Eire, is only about 150m (457ft) away. As the truck passed a medieval tower (Narrow Water Castle) by the side of the road, terrorists across the lough detonated an explosive device under the vehicle. The radio-controlled explosion killed a company commander and 15 soldiers from the Parachute Regiment and two from the Queen's Own Highlanders.

The commanding officer of the Queen's Own Highlanders, Lieutenant-Colonel Blair, immediately flew to Warrenpoint. As the helicopter landed he ran towards the carnage, at which point the terrorists detonated another device. The explosion vapourized his body.

The SAS in Northern Ireland

Bringing the SAS into a country whose history of "troubles" goes back as far as the 1920s has since been considered a mistake. In 1968, the civil-rights disturbances in Belfast resulted in volatile emotions and flared tempers. In April 1969 the Belfast government, alarmed by the violence between Protestants and Catholics, fuelled in part by the IRA, asked Westminster to provide military aid. In August 1969 British troops were sent to the Province and were welcomed by the Catholic population of Ulster. However, the troops misused their position by raiding several Catholic areas and using unnecessary force to disperse crowds, actions which caused their unpopularity and which culminated in the shooting of 13 Catholics on "Bloody Sunday" in 1972.

In Northern Ireland the Protestant Loyalists are the undoubted majority and the Catholic Nationalists, who want British rule to end and reunification with southern Ireland, the minority. However, the Loyalists realized that if the British

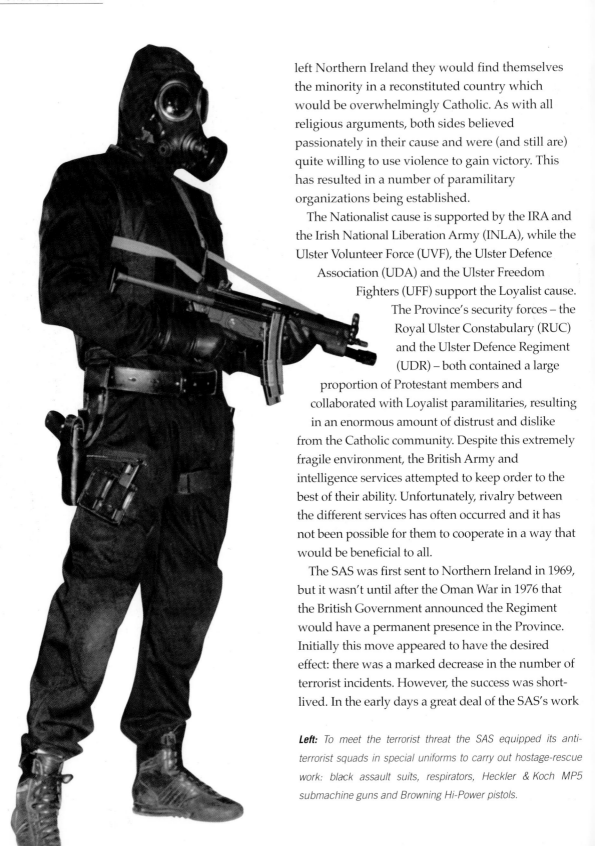

left Northern Ireland they would find themselves the minority in a reconstituted country which would be overwhelmingly Catholic. As with all religious arguments, both sides believed passionately in their cause and were (and still are) quite willing to use violence to gain victory. This has resulted in a number of paramilitary organizations being established.

The Nationalist cause is supported by the IRA and the Irish National Liberation Army (INLA), while the Ulster Volunteer Force (UVF), the Ulster Defence Association (UDA) and the Ulster Freedom Fighters (UFF) support the Loyalist cause. The Province's security forces – the Royal Ulster Constabulary (RUC) and the Ulster Defence Regiment (UDR) – both contained a large proportion of Protestant members and collaborated with Loyalist paramilitaries, resulting in an enormous amount of distrust and dislike from the Catholic community. Despite this extremely fragile environment, the British Army and intelligence services attempted to keep order to the best of their ability. Unfortunately, rivalry between the different services has often occurred and it has not been possible for them to cooperate in a way that would be beneficial to all.

The SAS was first sent to Northern Ireland in 1969, but it wasn't until after the Oman War in 1976 that the British Government announced the Regiment would have a permanent presence in the Province. Initially this move appeared to have the desired effect: there was a marked decrease in the number of terrorist incidents. However, the success was short-lived. In the early days a great deal of the SAS's work

Left: To meet the terrorist threat the SAS equipped its anti-terrorist squads in special uniforms to carry out hostage-rescue work: black assault suits, respirators, Heckler & Koch MP5 submachine guns and Browning Hi-Power pistols.

Above: The secret to SAS success is constant practice until drills become second nature. Five SAS soldiers wearing respirators, firing simultaneously, can acquire head shots up to a range of 600m (1968ft) without fail.

was simply to patrol the fields of South Armagh, but as the troubles progressed the SAS's role was expanded. In the 1970s, for example, a substantial number of successes were achieved as a result of intense surveillance work. Following numerous SAS ambushes as a result of this surveillance, many IRA and INLA terrorists were either killed or captured.

In 1973, shortly after the Munich Olympic Games massacre, the heads of government attending the G7 talks discussed the proposal to set up special anti-terrorist units in secret. In Great Britain the SAS was tasked with equipping and training a new force, known by a variety of names including the Anti-Terrorist Team, Special Patrol (SP) Team and the Pagoda Team. New equipment was purchased and the SAS responded to the training with unmatched keenness. Unknowingly it was to become the world's finest counter-terrorism unit, setting a standard that all others would be judged by.

CHAPTER 2

What is the Anti-Terrorist Team?

At any one time there is an SAS Sabre Squadron on 24-hour-stand-by for anti-terrorist and hostage-rescue operations: 64 men split into four 16-man teams ready to deal with any situation that may present itself. Each man is trained to perfection to carry out his task.

In 1973 the SAS officially formed its own Counter-Revolutionary Warfare (CRW) Cell, with the special purpose of developing techniques to counter terrorism. From its inception CRW was a vision of how the modern-day SAS soldier was to excel. No longer would he always fight in military clothing. CRW tasking called for civilian attire, and a variety of new weapons for covert missions. Surveillance and close-quarter battle techniques were combined with high-speed driving. New shooting skills were developed for hostage-rescue operations, being perfected in the so-called "Killing House" training centre.

The new SAS unit initially took on the title of Special Patrol (SP) Team, and it grew almost overnight. The new role required new equipment. SAS personnel were therefore sent directly to the Rover vehicle factory, where they took possession of the next four white Range Rovers coming off the production line. Rumours that the prime minister himself had ordered such direct action in the setting

Left: Members of the SAS Anti-Terrorist Team pose with one of the Regiment's Range Rover vehicles. Note that many sport the moustache that is the hallmark of an SAS soldier.

Above: The first Special Patrol Team was set up at the request of the then British prime minister Edward Heath. This photograph dates from the mid-1970s.

Above: The original Special Patrol Team had four white Range Rovers. Most of the early SAS anti-terrorist exercises began with a scramble and high-speed run to the incident site.

up and procurement of specialist equipment were basically true. The team grew rapidly, and eventually came to be a full squadron commitment – some 64 men (all squadrons are rotated through CRW duties). I think it is fair to say that it was this combination of the SP teamwork, mixed with the CRW training for Northern Ireland, that established the SAS in the anti-terrorist role for which it has become so renowned. At the same time, though, it would be wrong to assume that this was the Regiment's only commitment. Even though such actions as the Mogadishu hijack (1977) and the Iranian Embassy siege (1980) gripped the world's headlines, the SAS had its feet firmly on the ground. Anti-terrorist work was only part of its role; the wars in Oman (1970–76) and the Falklands (1982) were fought with equal enthusiasm.

This constant engagement in conflict is what makes the SAS soldier so respected and utterly competent. As the anti-terrorist role developed during the early 1970s, the old image of the SAS soldier as a jungle fighter (because of the conflicts in Malaya and Borneo) started to change. While

wars and small individual operations came and went, the SP Team and its work in Northern Ireland developed into a permanent commitment which remains to this day.

It was Captain Andrew Massey, who joined the SAS as a troop captain in 1971, who was the officer responsible for devising the outline concept of the British anti-terrorist team. He was asked by the colonel of the Regiment to write a paper on the concept. Massey went on to become colonel of the SAS, and during the 1991 Gulf War he was promoted to brigadier. He also served as Deputy Director of Special Forces. It was Massey who gathered A, D and B Squadrons together in the Gulf, the strongest concentration of SAS troops since World War II, and announced General Schwarzkopf's decision to use them inside Iraq. Brigadier Massey was well respected by his soldiers and renowned for his personal approach when addressing his men.

The transport for the first SP Team consisted of four white Range Rovers and four black Austin cars. The latter were very heavy and were soon disposed of in favour of more Range Rovers, which endure with the anti-terrorist team to this day. The equipment, by comparison to what is used today, was also very basic. The teams had plain black overalls (not flame-retardant) with normal waist holsters and no body armour. There were no such things as assault boots, and so for footwear most team members wore commercial training shoes for speed and adhesion. Only the weaponry was new. Although the assault team still used the Browning 9mm Hi-Power pistol, much favoured by the SAS for over 30 years, they had access to the new

Heckler & Koch MP5 submachine gun. Likewise, the sniper team still used the British Army-issue bolt-action L42 rifle. They also had access to the 7.62mm Tikka Finlander for short-range work. By today's standards we must have looked a motley crew. However, training went ahead with a vengeance. As techniques progressed, so the deficiencies in equipment became apparent and

Below: An early SAS anti-terrorist sniper. Though this shot is posed, it shows the rudimentary nature of the Regiment's anti-terrorist clothing at this time: overalls and no body armour.

Above: The Tikka Finlander was the first specialist sniper rifle issued to the SAS Anti-Terrorist Team. It was to be one of the first in a long line of SAS counter-terrorist hardware.

mechanical ingenuity became a necessity. Many of the skills learnt while operating in Northern Ireland, such as storming a house or ambushing a vehicle, were adopted and modified to fit hostage-rescue work. What no one had worked out, though, was how to assault a commercial aircraft, and in the early 1970s hijackings were still very much in favour with several terrorist organizations.

The best way to learn something like this is at an airport, and where better than Heathrow? In the early days of the SP Team the SAS had a great working relationship with the "Hard Dog" section stationed at Heathrow. This police unit, which was housed next to the main Heathrow police station, was primarily responsible for day-to-day security at Great Britain's premier airport. The liaison with the SAS worked extremely well, and many of the basic requirements for anti-hijack drills were learnt as a result. The dog section would arrange visits for small groups of SAS personnel, who would take advantage of the access to commercial aircraft. This

gave team members a chance to check on the different internal configurations of individual airliners. Door heights were measured, and all access points explored. It didn't take long to realize that it is possible to get on board most aircraft unseen. For example, most aircraft doors and escape hatches can be opened quickly using simple methods. Exercises on aircraft and buildings continued, and as each new challenge was encountered so a drill or piece of equipment was developed to overcome it. Ladders were manufactured that could be adjusted to almost any size, communications became smoother, and the whole anti-terrorist scenario started to take form.

A tour of duty with the SP Team (soon to be renamed the Anti-Terrorist Team) became part of the cycle for all SAS soldiers, who by the early 1970s were operating full-time in Northern Ireland and fighting a full-scale war in Oman. Anti-terrorist methods used in Northern Ireland differed very little from those used on the mainland, save for the fact that SAS members in Northern Ireland would normally operate in camouflage uniform or civilian clothes rather than black overalls.

Team Organization and Operating Methods

The SAS Anti-Terrorist Team comprises a command-and-control element, including specialist signals and intelligence operators, together with assault teams and sniper units. In addition, there is a back-up unit that provides the methods of entry (MOE). Assault personnel focus primarily on techniques of closing with and neutralizing the enemy. Snipers, on the other hand, would deal with any long-range situation that may present itself. This said, and although the two teams exercise independently, a lot of cross-training goes on, thus providing the numbers to suit the situation required. All members of the SAS Anti-Terrorist Team spend hundreds of hours in the now famous

"Killing House". This purpose-built, flat-roofed block building in the grounds of the SAS base, just behind the old Quartermaster's stores, is unique. From the moment the building was completed, it has been in constant daily use, not only by the Anti-Terrorist Team practising room assaults but also by the CRW Cell training men in bodyguard drills.

The SAS became good through hard work, innovative skills and by developing pioneering procedures. Specialist training had its drawbacks, however. At one stage, for example, the Regiment was in constant demand as the venue for VIP visits, all of them time-consuming. Through such visits many of the VIPs realized how advanced the SAS had become, and consequently many of their personal bodyguards were sent to Hereford for training. This diverted both time and resources away from fighting terrorism.

What was the procedure if a terrorist incident occurred on the mainland? Out of work hours, each

Below: VIPs have long made their way to the SAS "Killing House" to experience hostage-rescue drills. Here, Prince Charles and Princess Diana witness SAS skills at close quarters.

individual was issued with a recall device that had a range of about 48km (30 miles). When this was activated, members would make their way back to the SP Team hangar and make ready their vehicles. A quick briefing was normally given by the team commander or the SAS operations officer prior to the arrival of a police car escort, that would then accompany us all the way to the incident area. In the early days the team would either drive to the incident area or, if the distance exceeded three hours of driving, we would fly by C-130 Hercules to the nearest airport. Driving was great fun, as it inevitably involved a high-speed race up the M4 motorway from Herefordshire with a police escort. As we passed through the various counties local police units would join our convoy. Unfortunately, this did little more than attract unwanted public attention, especially on one occasion when the team almost ran down workers leaving their factory.

When we approached the incident site we would be directed to a holding area. Here we would lay out our equipment and prepare for an Immediate Action (IA). This was done to counter any threat from the terrorists, who might suddenly decide to

start shooting hostages. The IA plan would be very simple: close with the terrorists as quickly as possible and kill them, saving as many of the hostages as possible.

All these procedures were practised during the many exercises carried out by the SAS. Most exercises were primarily designed to train the SAS and police, but some were large-scale and involved government ministers, who also needed to experience the problems related to a terrorist attack against Great Britain. The Cabinet Office Briefing Room (COBRA) is an office where members of the British Government, senior police officers and military commanders meet in order to discuss major terrorist incidents. The SAS Director is

usually on hand to voice the options available that the Regiment can offer, and to keep COBRA fully informed as to the SAS's overall preparedness.

Commitment of the SAS to a terrorist incident is done through a series of procedures that have evolved since the Regiment was first introduced to the role of counter-terrorism. In Great Britain it is the police who have primacy, that is to say they are in charge of administrating the laws of the country. However, it was recognized that certain situations may occur where the police were unable to successfully assault a heavily armed and well-trained terrorist group. In such situations the chief constable governing the area where the incident has taken place will send a request to the Home Office for the SAS to intervene. This does not mean that they go immediately to the incident and take over; the police remain very much in charge. It does mean, however, that the SAS is on site and ready

Below: *With police primacy in Great Britain, SO19 is normally the first armed response on the ground following a terrorist incident. SO19 usually controls the outer perimeter.*

for any emergency that might occur. In practice what happens is that the police chief constable will telephone SAS headquarters directly and put the Regiment on stand-by, prior to asking official authorization from the Home Office.

Chief constables are regularly invited to a two-day seminar at the SAS base in Herefordshire. This serves to update the police on what is available and also to form a common rapport between the police and the SAS. Even when the SAS has been officially authorized and sent to the incident site, it does not go into action before the police issues a formal signed document giving the SAS control of the incident. This is not usually done until a few minutes prior to the actual assault. But how do SAS personnel get to the terrorist scene?

Transport

For normal day-to-day work the SAS uses Range Rovers. These robust cross-country vehicles have been used since the Anti-Terrorist Team was formed. The characteristics of the Range Rover, which at the time was only a year old, were ideally suited to the role. For example, the drop-down tailgate allowed for easy loading and the vehicle

Above: The C-130 Hercules transport aircraft of the RAF's Special Forces Flight can carry up to three fully laden Land Rovers plus their crews. This Hercules was used to transport SAS soldiers to Saudi Arabia during the 1991 Gulf War.

Below: New sniper control systems allow the SAS team commander to see what the sniper sees, thus enabling him to keep abreast of any developments during a siege. All snipers are trained to fire at a target's head to ensure an instant kill.

Above: Simple diversions can be extremely effective during an assault. This truck was set on fire to distract the terrorists during GSG 9's assault at Mogadishu in 1977.

itself could be used in an assault. Some 25 years on and the Range Rover is still used by the SAS, having been adapted as a main assault delivery vehicle. Platforms and ladders attached to the Range Rovers can carry assault personnel directly to the required height of an aircraft door or building window. While not in use, the vehicles are always parked in such a manner that the heavy equipment they carry to any incident can be instantly loaded.

All the vehicles are fitted with multi-frequency police radios, enabling them to talk to any police organization throughout the country. Car-to-car radios as well as normal telephone communications are also fitted. Certain police forces receive a special licence from the Home Office to exceed normal speed limits while instructing the SAS in high-speed driving techniques (roll bars are now fitted to SAS Land Rovers as standard after a number of high-speed accidents where vehicles left the road and crashed).

When the Anti-Terrorist Team is required to move to the outer reaches of Great Britain or carry out assignments overseas, they are transported by a

Special Forces Flight. There are two Special Forces Flights within the Royal Air Force (RAF), forming part of 7 and 47 Squadrons respectively, and both are dedicated to support army and Royal Marine special-operations units. Air crews within both flights are trained for special operations, specifically low-level deep penetration into enemy airspace and the delivery and extraction of special forces units.

Special Forces Flights

The Special Forces Flight of 7 Squadron is based at RAF Odiham in Hampshire. It is currently equipped with the UK-designated HC.2 variant of the Boeing Vertol Chinook twin-rotor heavy-lift helicopter, which can be fitted with four (two forward and two aft) M134 pintle-mounted miniguns. In the immediate future, however, the flight will be re-equipped with the HC.3 variant, which will be the first special operations-dedicated aircraft to be purchased by the British armed forces. The same aircraft, currently operated as the MH-47E by the US Army's 160th Aviation Battalion (better known as Task Force 160), features a glass cockpit, terrain-following Forward-Looking Infra-Red (FLIR) systems, built-in fast-roping brackets, and four .50-calibre Gecal miniguns.

The Special Forces Flight of 47 Squadron is located at RAF Lyneham in Wiltshire. It is equipped with the C-130K variant (designated C.3 in the UK) of the Hercules transport aircraft fitted with an in-flight refuelling probe, electronic countermeasures systems and chaff and flare dispensers, the dispensers providing a measure of defence against enemy air-defence systems.

The aircraft are currently being equipped with dedicated night-vision goggle (NVG) compatible cockpit lighting. It is reported that four of the C-130J Hercules on order for the RAF will be for dedicated special forces use, being upgraded to the same specification as the MC-130E Combat Shadow operated by the special operations squadrons of the US Air Force. This aircraft has terrain-following radar and FLIR systems, an integrated avionics package for long-range, low-level covert operations, enabling precision insertion and resupply of special forces, and NVG-compatible cockpit lighting. Finally, M Flight of the Royal Navy Fleet Air Arm's 848 Squadron, equipped with the Commando Mk.4 variant of the Westland Sea King helicopter, provides support for the maritime counter-terrorist role.

Satellite communications systems currently form part of the range of equipment accompanying the Anti-Terrorist Team when on overseas operations. They include static, mobile and portable units, the

Below: The author demonstrates an alternative use for a pistol during a simulated aircraft assault. Barry Davies took part in the Mogadishu rescue in 1977, when he stormed a Boeing 737.

Above: The SAS holds a comprehensive computer database that contains detailed information on the entry points of all makes of aircraft currently in use around the world.

latter weighing less than 22kg (48lb), operating on UHF and SHF frequency bands.

The SAS currently uses a number of Skynet 4 and 5 series satellites, which are in geosynchronous orbit, providing constant communications links worldwide. Once a transmitter/receiver has been set up and activated, it will locate and track a satellite with its dish antenna. Signals are transmitted on one frequency to the satellite, which transfers it to another frequency via a transponder, boosting the signal and re-transmitting it directly back to the secure communications unit at SAS headquarters in Great Britain.

When a terrorist incident occurs, it is imperative to contain it within a confined area to allow the SAS Anti-Terrorist Team to deploy. In most situations the incident will have been reported to the authorities, and the police will then have responded to confirm the event. Where the call is from a specific person, such as an airline pilot whose plane has been hijacked, a police response team will be put on stand-by and directed accordingly. In all cases once the nature of the incident has been established, or it is known at what airport the hijacked aircraft will land, an initial security perimeter will be put in place to contain the incident. A focal point will also be established known as the Forward Control Point (FCP). This can be either a commandeered building or a police mobile support unit.

The FCP will try to secure initial links (telephone or radio) directly with the terrorists to establish any demands, and to calm the immediate situation. The commander on the spot will also make sure that no one can enter or leave the incident area. Perimeter control of a major terrorist incident in Great Britain normally involves deploying the police unit identified as SO19. The original armed police anti-terrorist team which accompanied the SAS during early terrorist operations were marksmen from the D11 section. This police section was equipped and armed in a similar manner to the SAS, but dealt with matters deemed not to require specialized SAS talents. In the event of a terrorist incident where the Home Office requested the SAS, D11 normally remained on site to assist in the handling of the situation. D11 has now been replaced with the firearms section of the National Crime Unit – SO19.

SO19 will not only contain the incident area but will also deploy snipers, who in turn will update the FCP on all movements within the incident area. It is normal for the incident commander to order the local police to establish a second, outer cordon in order to prevent members of the public,

especially the "media circus", from getting too close. Somewhere within the inner cordon and normally close to the FCP, a place will be allocated to the SAS called the "holding area". The holding

Below: The Heckler & Koch MP5 submachine gun is the primary assault weapon of the SAS Anti-Terrorist Team. This is the shortened version of the weapon.

Below: The other weapon integral to SAS anti-terrorist work is the Browning Hi-Power pistol. Weighing only 0.9kg (2lb), it has a 14-round magazine and a range of 40m (131ft).

area should be large enough to house at least six Range Rovers and a large lorry. Thus it has to be similar in size to a small factory or warehouse. Rapid vehicle access is required, and there should be enough room for the men to lay out their equipment. In addition, it should be large enough to brief the whole team. In city areas finding a suitable holding area can be difficult, while airports offer several good options. In either case security from both the terrorists and the media is vital (it is assumed that the terrorists are listening to radios and watching television). The holding area will also house the support entry team, which is responsible for setting up the ladder

Above: *The CT12 respirator protects the wearer against smoke and gas. The respirator noseguard guides inhaled air up the sides of the face to minimize "fogging".*

Left: *Assault speed is everything. Ladders mounted on vehicles allow SAS teams to close with the terrorists as quickly as possible.*

systems and abseiling equipment. This team will also check and make ready any wall-breaching equipment required.

SAS Command & Control

The command-and-control element of the SAS Anti-Terrorist Team basically plans the operation based on the information to hand. The FCP, SO19 and the SAS snipers gather this information once they have been deployed. Several SAS signallers are also present to make sure the communications systems are functioning as required. They will be responsible for supplying any covert surveillance devices from a huge array of equipment currently available to the SAS. Sieges and hijacks often last days, which means battery charging and back-up are also the signallers' responsibility, as is setting up the satellite system.

The briefing area is set up by men from the SAS intelligence unit. Their task is to see that all information is made available and that the team members can easily see it. Some information will be retrieved from enormous databases held by the SAS, which can include the layout of aircraft seating, important building plans, and information on individual terrorist groups. Originally, briefings for the team would take place on a large magnetic board that detailed a ground plan of the aircraft or building to be assaulted.

Coloured buttons representing members of the team, hostages and terrorists were placed or moved as plans and information were acquired. It was a good way of showing everyone where the hostages and terrorists were, and where the SAS should be prior to any assault. Compared to modern-day methods of briefing, though, it was crude. The SAS

Right: *SAS anti-terrorist clothing is black for a reason – the sinister appearance gives individual soldiers a psychological edge during a hostage-rescue operation.*

now has access to software modules designed specifically for operations, contingency and emergency planning. Developed over a number of years through associations with various police forces and special operations units, the software provides both planning and real-time control for any type of major incident, especially counter-terrorism. Gone are the days when the Anti-Terrorist Team would sit around while the operations personnel used sticky tape to hold up a plan of a building or hijacked aircraft. All that has been replaced with computerized visualization of what can or will happen. In addition to its massive capabilities in the pre-planning of incidents and

events, the software has considerable features available which permit planning and control in "real time". Consequently, the spontaneous and the unforeseen are dealt with as they happen. The basic sequence of events of most terrorist incidents can be pre-planned and loaded into the system.

Old operations, both successful and unsuccessful, are registered in the database and used as reference points. For example, if there is a hijacked Boeing 777 at Heathrow Airport, the Anti-Terrorist Team would have immediate access to the airport plans. The operators can even construct a three-dimensional computer model of the aircraft which can be viewed from any angle. Internal layouts of individual buildings and all aircraft types can also be stored in the system.

Computer-Aided Plans

Computer technology allows the SAS to plan for terrorist incidents before they happen. For example, pre-planned aircraft parking allocation and sniper locations at all major British airports help reduce the time required to place the team in a position to assault. By utilizing highly detailed graphic displays, the system presents realistic images of plans, operational data, mapping, photographs, video clips, text instructions, full-event logging and three-dimensional models. The latter allow for an animated "walk-through" by the team commander, making sure that everyone is familiar with where he should go during an assault. The current software is called Atlas Ops, and it is truly one of the finest tools serving the command-and-control elements of counter-terrorist units.

The team commanders will form a liaison with the police incident commander and the police

Left: *Stoppage and reloading drills are practised constantly to minimize the risks of an assault failing. The weapon here is a Heckler & Koch MP5K submachine gun.*

negotiator, and in many cases these men will know each other from the seminars held at SAS headquarters. The team commander will want to collate every last bit of information from the negotiator, as he is the man in direct contact and proximity to the terrorists. The team commander will want to know everything, such as the terrorists' mood, number of hostages, even door structures and number of windows. Most of all, the team commander will explore any avenue that, in the event of an assault, will lead to a swift and successful end.

Diversions

Diversions are a vital part of any assault and normally happen just prior to the team going in. The type of diversion used can vary from a simple telephone conversation, as used in the Iranian Embassy siege in London in 1980, to exploding a fuel truck, as hostage-rescue forces did during the aircraft hijack at Mogadishu in 1977. Prior to the Moluccan train siege in 1977, Dutch fighter aircraft flew over the carriages with full afterburners ignited. All these diversions serve to illustrate how terrorists can be distracted according to the individual situation preceding any assault. Once the assault has been initiated, the assault teams themselves require additional diversionary tactics. By this time the terrorists are fully aware that something is happening, and any distraction needs to be very aggressive.

The British company Royal Enfield Ordnance, at the request of the SAS, experimented with various distraction devices and the one that seemed most decisive was the G60 stun grenade. The device produces loud noise (160 decibels) combined with

Right: The weapons for members of the SAS Anti-Terrorist Team are carried to the scene in cases to protect their working parts from dust and water. They are unloaded at the last moment.

Above: Powerful torches can be mounted on weapon barrels to allow team members to see during an assault. Electricity is normally cut prior to the assault.

high light output (300,000 candle-light) without any harmful fragmentation. It is capable of stunning anyone in close proximity for a period of around 3–5 seconds when detonated, and is one of the most effective items in the anti-terrorist armoury. The effect is not dissimilar to the flashing strobes in a disco, but a million times more disorientating. Also called a "flash-bang", this effective device has become essential in almost all hostage-rescue scenarios.

Originally developed for the SAS Regiment, it has now become a standard item in many of the world's counter-terrorism squads. It contains a mixture of magnesium powder and fulminate of mercury,

which detonates once the ring is pulled and the grenade is thrown. The grenade bodies are constructed with a minimum of metal parts to ensure that there is no danger of hostages being injured by fragmentation. They were used for the first time operationally during the Mogadishu hijack, where three were thrown just prior to the assault after a fuel truck had been set on fire. During the Iranian Embassy siege it is thought that one of the grenades set fire to a curtain, although this was never proved, resulting in the building subsequently being gutted by fire.

Screening

Where the assault team is forced to cross open ground prior to any assault, it is possible to put in place a large-area smoke screen. This helps reduce casualties and guarantees more assault personnel reaching the target. An effective smoke screen can conceal the size and disposition of assaulting forces, allowing them to manoeuvre under cover and close to the terrorist location. Large areas of impenetrable smoke can also be used as diversions, confusing the terrorists. Smoke obscuration is particularly valuable prior to an aircraft attack, where the assault vehicles must cross open distances to gain access to the aircraft's doors. The latest smoke generator comes mounted on a small truck and is capable of rapid smoke production over a wide area. The one disadvantage with a smoke screen is that it alerts terrorists that an assault is imminent.

Much has been written about the swiftness of the SAS during their assaults, with justifiable reason. The SAS learnt many years ago that both speed and aggression play a major role in any successful assault. The basic instinct of survival is strong in all

Right: SAS team members are trained to use all possible entry points. Rubber-soled boots ensure that abseilers are not heard until they crash through the windows.

human beings, including those who are prepared to die for their cause. While the terrorists point guns at their hostages, threatening them with death, they are in control. However, the moment they are faced with figures dressed in black and confronting them with imminent death, the situation changes. No matter how dedicated the terrorist, he or she will ignore the hostages and concentrate on the immediate threat to his or her own life. Unfortunately for the terrorist, the man in black has superior training, state-of-the-art weaponry and body protection. There is at this stage no contest other than one of speed.

Closing with the enemy is vital; the quicker it can be achieved the greater are the chances of success. Moreover, any further risks to the hostages are minimized. Speed can be achieved through swift delivery of the assault team to where it can gain immediate access to the incident site. This can be either the windows or doors of a building or the doors of an aircraft. In addition, there must be minimum delay in breaching the incident site – doors, walls and windows must be opened instantly. And assault members must locate and physically close the distance to the point where any terrorist threat can be neutralized. Selecting multi-entry points will help guarantee a successful assault. Ultimately, however, the success of a hostage-rescue operation depends on the personal skills of those carrying out the assault.

Close-quarter battle (CQB) is a method of fighting that the SAS has developed since the early 1960s. It has two forms: armed and unarmed. Armed CQB covers a wide range of pistol and submachine gun techniques. Weapons training starts from the very basics of pistol work and encompasses all the

Left: Body armour is a double-edged weapon. While it protects the SAS man against enemy gunfire, it is bulky and can restrict the wearer's movement during an assault.

problems of movement and weapons stoppages. It then progresses to more advanced techniques using automatic weaponry, rolling movements, and both primary and secondary weapons. At this stage the basic moves – kneeling, turning and rolling – are incorporated. At the same time the famous SAS "double tap" is taught, which basically involves firing two shots in rapid succession to the torso of the target. It takes several years to become comfortable with this method of shooting, but the results have proved themselves over and over again: two rounds stop a terrorist better than one. The next level comes with progression to the Heckler & Koch MP5 submachine gun.

Below: Close Quarter Battle teaches team members all the refinements of SAS shooting skills. Contrary to popular myth, SAS soldiers are not trained to fire from the hip.

Above: Range work is a daily commitment for both snipers and members of the assault teams. Constant practice is the secret of the Anti-Terrorist Team's success.

This weapon is the backbone of the anti-terrorist soldier and is used by just about every country in the world. What makes the MP5 so special is its compactness, its ability to produce three separate modes of fire – single shot, three-round burst and full-automatic – and its reliability (it rarely jams). The SAS normally shuns weapon slings as being cumbersome, but the MP5 is the only weapon where it is utilized. The reason for this is based on the need to have the weapon securely attached around the body while the pistol is being used.

The final stage of weapons training is to use both MP5 and pistol together. This incorporates practising stoppage drills on either of the weapons while using the other as an immediate back-up. While all SAS soldiers learn stoppage drills, clearing a stoppage in the middle of an actual assault requires too much time, and therefore it is safer to transfer immediately to a back-up weapon

if the main weapon jams (seconds count during a hostage rescue).

Constant training is the key to creating excellent hostage-rescue personnel. For example, on average each member of the team fires around 2000 rounds of ammunition a week on one range or another. The training is intense, and is designed so soldiers are able to identify, hit and kill a target in under three

Below: An SAS Anti-Terrorist Team poses for the camera. In less than 30 years the SAS has established itself as the best counter-terrorist unit in the world.

seconds. The new facility is extremely sophisticated, to the point where both the Germans and Americans have copied it. From basic weapon handling SAS students move on to a variety of hostage-rescue scenarios including the "snatch" (see Chapter 7). This is a drill which is practised as part of the anti-terrorist hostage-rescue situation. It involves going into a room shrouded in darkness, in which a live hostage is to be found seated among several paper targets. The paper targets are shredded by automatic fire while the terrified "hostage" sits rooted to the spot.

CQB instruction in unarmed combat is fast and deadly, though relatively simple. It includes learning about the defensive and offensive parts of the body, and how best to use them or protect against them. Something as simple as a rolled-up newspaper jabbed into the solar plexus can take an opponent down, as can a fist weighted with a handful of coins. In many cases the SAS is required to carry out a "hard" arrest (not killing the suspect), sometimes against an enemy known to be armed. CQB provides the techniques by which this can be quickly and safely done.

CHAPTER 3

Hostage-Rescue Scenarios

By the late 1970s, the Anti-Terrorist Team was a highly trained unit. But how would it perform in action? The answer was provided in May 1980, when terrorists seized the Iranian Embassy. Before the world's cameras, the team demonstrated it was a true élite.

Terrorists can attack in any number of ways, though normally they do so in ways that are both savage and media-seeking. They may take hostages and hold them to ransom, or may simply murder by bomb or bullet. It really depends on the situation and what the terrorist organization is trying to achieve. If the attack is a reprisal, then it is almost certainly going to be a bombing or shooting incident. If the organization is looking to have fellow prisoners released from jail or have its grievances recognized by the world at large, then hostage-taking is the usual approach. To prevent such actions taking place, security forces monitor most terrorist organizations in order to anticipate any future actions they may be planning. Where the terrorists have accomplished a bombing or shooting, of course, the security forces can only react retrospectively. Only when prior information about a terrorist attack is obtained can counter-measures be initiated to prevent or limit the damage caused by such an incident. Anti-terrorist units prepare for a number of assault options:

Left: Monday 5 May 1980 – the SAS Anti-Terrorist Team storms the Iranian Embassy in London and enters popular mythology.

aircraft assault, building assault, vehicle assault (including trains and coaches) and seaborne assault (including ships and oil rigs). Outline contingency plans for all these events already exist, and most can be modified to a specific incident.

Immediate Action

In any response to a terrorist incident, time is a key factor. The time span is normally dictated by how long it would take to implement the terrorist demands. At the very least this will run into several hours, and with a viable delaying policy in place this can be extended to a number of days. The delay provides the Anti-Terrorist Team with enough time to deploy into a position, where at the very least it can protect the lives of hostages or property. The Immediate Action (IA) plan is the most basic level of operational planning. Depending on the situation, it is put into force the moment the team is assembled in the holding area. It is only activated in an emergency, i.e. prior to a full-scale detailed assault plan being available.

To my knowledge the only time an IA has been used was during the hijacking of an Air France Airbus on 24 December 1994. At midday, French television gave news of a hijack that had taken place at Algiers Airport. It reported that an Air France Airbus had been boarded by four Islamic fundamentalists, who had taken the 220 passengers and 12 crew hostage. Shortly after, the terrorists released 19 people, mainly women and children.
However, this act of mercy was soon overshadowed when the terrorists shot and killed two hostages, an Algerian policeman and a Vietnamese diplomat. Hours later,

early on Christmas morning, they released more women and children, bringing the total to 63. A few hours later, a third hostage was shot: a 27-year-old Frenchman, a cook with the French Embassy in Algiers. Soon after, the aircraft was forced to take off, landing early next morning in Marseille.

What the general public did not realize is that the Air France Airbus was one of the worst hijack scenarios possible. With hostages being killed, an IA plan was called for. The élite French counter-terrorist group, the *Groupement d'Intervention de la Gendarmerie Nationale* (GIGN), had to get on board the aircraft as soon as possible to neutralize the terrorists and free the hostages. The risks to both the assault force and the hostages were very high, due to the lack of surprise or diversion. After the aircraft had landed at Marseille, the aircraft was immediately surrounded by snipers of the GIGN. Then, at 15:45 hours, the aircraft moved towards the control tower without permission. The

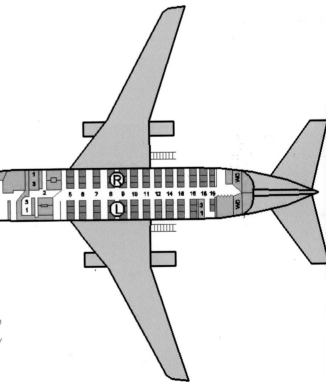

Right: The Boeing 737 is ideally suited to an assault. It is easy to enter, has only one aisle and any terrorists on board are usually easy to see and close with.

Above: GIGN personnel storm the hijacked Air France Airbus at Marseille Airport on 26 December 1994. The operation was a success, though several GIGN members were wounded.

Below: GIGN men after their assault at Marseille in 1994. GIGN is the only unit to date to have performed an Immediate Action when it freed the hostages from Arab extremists.

demands from the authorities for the aircraft to stop and move no farther were met with several shots at the control tower from the terrorists.

By this time the GIGN commander must have realized the terrorists' intentions and ordered the IA to be carried out. By 17:17 hours, assault units of the GIGN could be seen racing towards the rear of the aircraft, and sniper fire was heard. The team commander, Denis Favier, together with his second-in-command Olivier Kim, stormed the front right door. They used normal airport landing steps to gain entry, and despite trouble with the door the entry, considering the conditions, was very slick. At the same time Captain Tardy led another unit via the right rear door, using the same entry method. Once on board, both groups made their way towards the cockpit where most of the terrorists had gathered. A third group of GIGN personnel moved into position under the belly of the aircraft, ready to receive the hostages. Inside the aircraft the

Above: *The main problem with an assault against an aircraft is its size. The crucial factor is assault speed, which is naturally reduced in a large aircraft such as a Boeing 747 (seen here).*

two teams moved quickly, separating the terrorists from the hostages and disembarking the latter as soon as possible. By 17:39 hours the four terrorists lay dead. Although the hostages got away with a few minor cuts and bruises, the cost to GIGN and the crew was heavy. Nine GIGN were wounded, two quite severely, one lost two fingers and one was shot in the foot. The three members of the crew that were hurt had unfortunately been trapped with the terrorists in the cockpit area.

During the assault by GIGN the co-pilot managed to climb out of a small window and throw himself to the ground, and despite a broken leg managed to effect his escape. Later reports indicated that the terrorist plan was to fill the aircraft full of fuel and blow it up over Paris; this theory was enforced when 20 sticks of dynamite were found under the front- and mid-section seats.

The hijacking of an aircraft creates two distinct threats: the killing of hostages and the threat of converting the aircraft into a flying bomb. Most hijackings take place in the air, a modus operandi which favours the terrorists' chances of success. There is usually very little resistance to a mid-air hijack, mainly because the passengers are too scared and the crew are too busy flying the aircraft. In addition, any damage to the aircraft while in flight can produce fatal results. The standard terrorist procedure is to smuggle guns, grenades or explosives on board the aircraft and then use them to take command, using the threat of violence against the crew and passengers or, in the extreme, total aircraft destruction. Demands during aircraft hijacks are normally simple – "recognize that we are in charge and take us to wherever we want to go".

Owing to fuel considerations aircraft have limited flying time – they must eventually land. This is usually, although not always, done at an international airport. Once on the ground the situation changes, as it allows the Anti-Terrorist

Team an opportunity to assault the aircraft. If time permits, contingency plans are put into operation, diverting other aircraft and stopping the terrorists from changing aircraft. Additionally, snipers can be deployed to pre-arranged hides prior to the aircraft landing, and assault teams can prepare for an IA should the situation become unstable.

Any aircraft assault is divided into three parts: the approach, the entry, and the assault. With few exceptions an assault team can approach most aircraft from its blind area at the rear. A good team commander will know exactly what area he has to manoeuvre in. A silent approach allows the team to reach the outside of the fuselage undetected. Once

Below: An SAS drill during the late 1970s. As soon as they arrive at the terrorist incident, SAS soldiers will have an Immediate Action plan ready to free the hostages.

in position, ladders are placed against the doors and entry points prior to an entry being made. The size of the aircraft involved and the number of passengers onboard will dictate how many entry points the team needs to breach in order to make a successful entry.

Almost all aircraft doors, both normal passenger and emergency, can be opened from outside of the aircraft while it is on the ground. This is a design element which facilitates emergency services having access in the event of accident, crash or other emergency. Most aircraft, especially the larger types, require that the assault team be elevated several metres off the ground in order to gain access. A wide variety of ladder systems are thus available to the assaulting team. These can be adjusted to reach any type of aircraft door. In some cases, two ladders are used side by side and placed

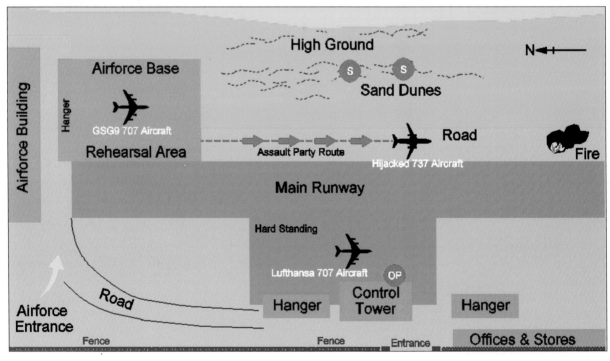

Top: *Assault ladders are an essential item in the SAS's hostage-rescue armoury. Lightweight, they have rubber pads for silent placement against the sides of an aircraft.*

Above: *The author's plan for the assault on the hijacked Lufthansa Boeing 737 at Mogadishu in October 1977. Note the diversionary fire started in front of the aircraft.*

against the aircraft fuselage, the idea being that the first man operates the handle and uses his body weight to swing the door open, the second man being free to fire or enter the moment the door is opened. Ladders are also used to gain access to the aircraft's wings, whereupon the emergency doors can be opened.

Until recently stealth has been the most popular method of assaulting hijacked aircraft. However, many anti-terrorist teams now favour a rapid-response vehicle. This vehicle has a pre-assembled platform system attached which can be adjusted to any height. The result is a modern mobile siege tower which transports the assaulting members at the correct elevation directly to the aircraft entry points. While the vehicles can still take advantage of the blind area located at the rear of the aircraft, they also offer a rapid delivery. It is incumbent on the team commander to get all his men onto the aircraft in order to facilitate a good assault, therefore the vehicle is normally armoured.

Aircraft Assaults

It is not possible to give details on all types of aircraft, as there are so many sizes and variations. However, my personal plan to assault flight LH181 (hijacked by Arab terrorists in October 1977) while on the ground in Dubai is a good example. The Boeing 737 is a simple little animal where anti-terrorist drills are concerned. There are only three options for entry: tail, wings and front catering area. I thought that if the terrorists began to carry out any threatened shootings, they would naturally take the precaution of covering the main doors. It seemed less likely that they would cover the two emergency exit doors leading on to the wings, so the plan that basically fell into shape was to attack through these entry points. The fact that the wing emergency exits were designed to be opened easily from the outside was another strong factor in

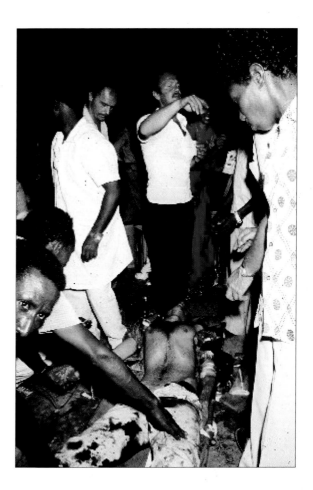

Above: Victory at Mogadishu. This photograph was taken moments after the successful assault by GSG 9 and shows the body of the terrorist leader.

favour of adopting this mode of attack, but there were others.

The West German anti-terrorist team, *Grenzschutzgrüppe* 9 (GSG 9), had also discovered a blind spot where the wing joins the aircraft body. Two men could sit beneath the emergency doors and not be visible from any of the windows. By comparison, the entry and exit points at the front and rear require considerable manhandling and some time to get them open. For instance, the front door is operable through a small hatch on the

outside of the aircraft, which allows the door to be opened and brought down and the stairs to extend automatically.

The basic moves involved in my plan were: (1) To make a single-file approach to the aircraft from its blind spot at the rear, assemble our ladders quietly and erect them to the wings and the rear door. (2) To put each of the two leading assault teams covertly on the wings – one outside the port emergency exit, the other outside the starboard – with the second assault pairs waiting on the top rungs of the ladders. Each of these assault teams consisted of an SAS man or a GSG 9 man, backed up by a soldier from the Dubai Palace Guard. The reason that we involved the Palace Guard in this way was purely political, the Dubai Government being unwilling to allow us to mount the assault unless they played a part. (3) To position back-up

Above: Like a modern-day siege tower, this vehicle has a top-mounted assault ladder to enable a hostage-rescue squad to move quickly to the target.

squads beneath the rear area of the plane ready to scale their ladders, open the rear door and effect their entry as quickly as possible. At the same time, a second back-up squad would move quietly forward until it was beneath the front door area, ready to erect its ladders and follow suit. The back-ups would coordinate their moves with those of the assault teams. (4) When everyone was in position and the "GO" order given, the leading assault teams were to stand, punch the emergency exit panels and drop the doors onto the laps of the passengers in the mid-section of the cabin. The teams would then enter, the port-side pair clearing to the front of the cabin, the starboard team clearing to the rear. The leading teams were to receive immediate back-up from the second assault pairs entering behind them from their stations at the tops of the ladders to maintain control of the centre of the aircraft. (5) Simultaneous with the assault, the outside squads were to open both front and rear doors and enter the plane. The intention here was to provide further back-up in case of any problems, and also provide routes for the hostages to leave the plane, which by this time would be full of smoke from the stun grenades. As I mentioned earlier, the 737 is a fairly simple aircraft.

Once entry had been effected to the centre of the aircraft, the starboard assault team would gain a clear line of sight to the toilet doors at the rear of the cabin. The port team, moving forward through the economy area, would arrive in the first-class section which leads into the front catering area. Directly beyond this is the flight deck, the door to which is usually closed. The only obstacles the team would encounter would be this door and the curtains that separated economy and first class. Although this basic plan was quite uncomplicated, we calculated that it would require a great deal of practice to get the timing right, particularly the time it would take the assault teams to effect their entry and make their way to the front and rear of the passenger cabin. I anticipated that as soon as we dominated these points, the only people in serious danger would be the crew in the cockpit. This plan worked well during rehearsals in Dubai, and was adapted for the final assault in Mogadishu.

Buildings

All building assaults pose the same problems: the number of floors involved, the number and distribution of hostages, and the number and distribution of terrorists. Getting close to a building is in most cases fairly easy, as is gaining access. The major problem rests with closing with the terrorists

Above: *Assault speed can only be achieved if all the obstacles between the team and the terrorists have been removed. One way of doing this is to use a thermic lance.*

Below: *Breaching walls has always been a problem for the Anti-Terrorist Team. Purpose-built frame charges mean that the team can blow holes through brick and concrete. Explosives can be wrapped in flexible foam so they can be bent to the desired shape.*

quickly enough to prevent them killing any hostages. The best-known building assault carried out by the SAS was at the Iranian Embassy in London in 1980, which stands as a prime example of an effective hostage-rescue operation. At 11:25 hours on the morning of Wednesday 30 April, six armed gunmen took over No 16 Princes Gate, the Iranian Embassy in London's Kensington district. The terrorists were ostensibly opposed to the regime of Ayatollah Khomeini, and were seeking the independence of an Arab-speaking Iranian region called Khuzestan, also known as Arabistan. As they took control of the embassy, they gained 26 hostages including the British policeman PC Trevor

Below: Building assaults require multi-entry techniques. In addition, assault speed is reduced by the need to clear the building room by room. This team is using a vehicle platform.

Lock, who had been on duty at the entrance to the building. This was something that might have gone unnoticed, but for the fact that Lock had managed to alert his headquarters before being taken by the terrorists and, minutes later, a burst of submachine-gun fire was heard from inside the building. The police were on the scene immediately.

Armed police D11 marksmen soon surrounded the building, and the siege negotiating plans were put into operation. By 11:47 hours, Dusty Grey, an ex-D Squadron SAS man, who at the time worked with the Metropolitan Police, was talking to the SAS Commanding Officer in Hereford. His information contained the briefest details, but it was enough to alert the Regiment. Several minutes later, the duty signaller activated the "call-in" bleepers carried by every member of the Anti-Terrorist Team (although the SAS had prior warning, there can be no move before official sanction from the Home Secretary, who at the request of the police will contact the Ministry of Defence (MoD); despite this red tape, it makes sense for the SAS to think ahead, and positioning the Anti-Terrorist Team closer to the scene can save time and lives).

The SAS Team Arrives

Around midnight on the first day, most of the team members had made their way to Regent's Park barracks, which had been selected as a holding area. From there, various pieces of information could be assembled and assessed. A scale model of No 16 Princes Gate was ordered to be made, a task which fell to two military engineers drafted in from the nearby Guards unit. In addition, an intelligence cell was set up to gather and collate every snippet of information that would aid an assault. By this time the terrorist leader, named Oan, had secured his 26 hostages and issued his demands. These included the autonomy and recognition of the

Above: The roof of the Iranian Embassy and adjacent buildings in London in 1980. The SAS team members had to be careful not to dislodge any slates as they were deploying.

Arabistan people and the release of 91 political prisoners. Despite several threats to blow up the embassy and kill the hostages, by Thursday 1 May the terrorists had released a sick woman. Later that same day, Oan had managed to get a telephone call through to Sadegh Ghotzbadeh, Iran's Foreign Minister. The conversation did not go well, though. Oan was accused of being an American agent, and told that the Iranian hostages held in the embassy would consider it an honour to die for their country and the Iranian revolutionary movement. Around this time Chris Cramer, a BBC sound man, became sick with acute stomach pains. His partner, BBC sound recordist Sim Harris, pleaded with Oan to call for a doctor immediately. This was done, but the police refused to comply and in the end Cramer was released, whereupon he stumbled out of the embassy door and into a waiting ambulance.

Later that night, again under the cover of darkness, three Avis rental vans pulled up in a small side street by Princes Gate. Men carrying holdalls quickly made their way into No 14, just two doors down from the embassy. Within minutes they had laid out their equipment and made ready for an IA. The IA plan was very simple. If the terrorists started shooting, the SAS teams would run to the front door of No 16 and beat their way in – a slow and primitive action but better than doing nothing until a clearly defined plan could be organized. By 06:00 hours on the morning of Friday 2 May, the situation inside No 16 was getting very agitated. Oan called on the telephone which had been set up between the embassy and No 25 Princes Gate – The Royal School of Needlework – which now housed Alpha Control (main forward control point) and the police negotiator. Oan's main criticism was that no news had been broadcast about the siege, so how could his cause be heard? By late afternoon on the same day, Oan was allowed to make a statement which was to be broadcast on the next news slot. In return for this two more hostages were released, one of whom was a pregnant woman. The trouble was Oan would not release the hostages before the statement was read out, but the police wanted the

Below: The primary assault on the Iranian Embassy in 1980 was launched from the roof. Here, SAS soldiers move into position prior to abseiling down the sides of the building.

Above: On the given command, three four-man SAS teams abseiled over the edge of the building and crashed through the second- and third-floor windows.

hostages first. In the end a compromise was reached, and the broadcast went out on the BBC's Nine o'Clock News.

Two hours later, eight members of the SAS team had climbed onto the rear roof of No 14 and were making their way amid a jungle of television antenna to No 16. Two of the men made their way directly to a glass skylight, and after some time managed to get it free. They found that it opened directly into a small bathroom on the top floor of the embassy, and would provide an excellent entry point. Meanwhile, other members secured ropes to the several chimneys and made ready for a quick

Right: The stun grenades thrown into the Iranian Embassy to disorientate the terrorists started a fire. One SAS soldier became entangled in his abseiling kit and was burned.

descent to the lower floors, where they could smash in through the windows. By 09:00 hours on Sunday morning things seemed to be heading for a peaceful settlement. Oan had agreed to reduce his demands, and at the same time Arab ambassadors had attended a COBRA (Cabinet Office Briefing Room) Committee meeting in Whitehall. This committee was chaired by the Home Secretary, William Whitelaw, who was to all intents and purposes in charge of the whole operation, deciding the path of any action. He was aware that the SAS Anti-Terrorist Team now had access into the embassy, and that all efforts were being made to penetrate one of its walls (various sound distractions supplied by the Gas Board working in the vicinity prevented the drilling from being heard).

Above: Once inside the embassy, the SAS soldiers had little difficulty sorting out the hostages from the terrorists, and the latter were speedily neutralized.

COBRA was also aware that a basic plan had been formalized. The plan involved attacking all floors simultaneously, with clearly defined areas of demarcation to avoid accidents. Mock-ups of the floor layouts were constructed from timber and hessian sheeting and assembled at Regent's Park barracks in order that the SAS could practice. The police, who had adopted a softly-softly negotiating approach, managed to keep control of the siege for several more days. Extra time was desperately needed for the SAS to carry out covert reconnaissance, study plans, build models and, more importantly, locate the hostages and terrorists within the embassy building. A major breakthrough was talking to the former hostage Chris Cramer, the BBC sound engineer. It was a big mistake by the terrorists to have let him go: in his debrief to the SAS he was able to give precise and detailed information about the situation inside the embassy.

"Go. Go. Go."

By the sixth day of the siege, 5 May, the terrorists were becoming frustrated and the situation inside the embassy began to deteriorate. All morning threats were made about executing hostages, and at 13:31 hours three shots were heard. At 18:50 hours more shots were heard, and the body of the embassy press officer was thrown onto the pavement. Immediately the police appeared to capitulate, stalling for time, while SAS plans to storm the embassy were advanced. At this stage the police negotiator worked hard to convince the terrorist leader not to shoot any further hostages, and that a bus would be with them shortly to take them to the airport, from there they could fly to the Middle East. During this telephone conversation, the SAS men took up their start positions. A hand-written note which passed control from the police to the SAS was handed over. Shortly after, while a negotiator from Alpha Control talked to Oan, the SAS moved in. Oan heard the first crashes and complained that the embassy was being attacked. (This conversation was recorded, and one can clearly hear the stun grenades going off. Oan's conversation was cut short by a long burst of submachine-gun fire.)

For the assault team the waiting was over; and the words guaranteed to send their adrenalin pumping were given: "Go. Go. Go." At 19:23 hours, eight men abseiled down to the first-floor balcony, with ropes secured from the embassy roof. The assault came from three directions, with the main

Above: The charred remains of one of the terrorists killed inside the Iranian Embassy. Five of the six terrorists were killed during the assault; two hostages were killed and another two wounded.

attack from the rear. Frame charges were quickly fitted to the windows (by now these devices had been perfected) and blown. Stun grenades were thrown into the building in advance of the assault teams, which then went into action. Systematically, the building was cleared from the top down, room by room. The telex room on the second floor ,which housed the male hostages and three of the terrorists, was of utmost priority.

Realizing that an assault was in progress, the terrorists shot and killed one hostage and wounded two others before the lead SAS team broke into the room. Immediately they shot two gunmen that were visible, the third hid among the hostages and was not discovered, and killed, until later. As rooms were cleared, hostages were literally thrown from one SAS soldier to another, down the stairs and out into the back garden. At this stage they were all laid

Above: Any anti-terrorist team approaching an oil rig must do so underwater to remain undetected. In Great Britain oil rig protection is the responsibility of the Special Boat Service.

face down on the ground while a search was conducted for the missing terrorist. Breaking the siege took just 17 minutes. The SAS took no casualties, other than one man who got caught up in his rope harness and was badly burnt when a curtain caught fire. Once the embassy had been cleared, and all the terrorists and hostages had been identified, the incident was handed back to the police. Meanwhile, the SAS men vacated No 14 and went back to Regent's Park barracks in time to watch themselves on television.

Still dressed in assault gear, and clutching cans of Fosters lager (someone was on the ball), they crowded around, eager to see themselves in action.

Halfway through Prime Minister Margaret Thatcher, who had left a dinner date, arrived personally to thank the SAS. She circulated, as one man put it, "Like a triumphant Caesar returning to the Senate", her face glowing with pride and admiration at her Imperial Guard. Then, as the news started to show the event, she sat down on the floor amidst her warriors and watched with them. In total there were 26 hostages taken when the siege started. Of these five were released before the SAS assault. Two died, but the remaining 19 survived. Of the six terrorists, only one survived.

In the unusual case of a ship tied up alongside a dock being hijacked, the situation will normally be treated in a similar way to a building assault. As

Below: As with oil rigs, the main problem with regard to a ship-at-sea assault is getting to the vessel unseen. Again, the best method is an underwater approach to the target.

with oil rigs a hijack at sea poses several problems, especially in matters of approach. A ship is isolated on a flat surface over which would-be terrorists can observe for several miles. This limits the element of surprise and gives the terrorists time to carry out retaliatory actions prior to any assault. In the past, Anti-Terrorist Team members have been dropped by parachute close to shipping, but this method of deployment is very hit and miss and dependent on the weather. A sub-surface assault offers the best approach. Underwater deployments with submarines, sub-skimmers (small one- or two-man submersible) or divers offer excellent covert delivery to the target. The problem of getting from the sea and onto the ship or rig superstructure has also been overcome.

Although oil rigs are extremely high, most have some form of ladder system which will allow access to the main superstructure. Access to ships with superstructures not too high above water level is accomplished using a special grapple and flexible ladder which is hoisted into position. On larger ships where the superstructure is very high, suction pads can be used to climb the outer surface (this can even be done while the ship is moving). Once the assault team has several members on board, flexible ladders will be released to enable others to climb aboard. The actual assault is carried out in a similar way to buildings, with each deck being cleared from the top down.

The main threat against both shipping and oil rigs is one of total destruction. A small motor-powered launch fitted with several tons of high explosive is enough to send either to the bottom of

Below: If terrorists seize a ship in port the tasks of an anti-terrorist squad is made much easier, and the assault will be treated in a similar way to a building assault.

the sea, and as yet there is no answer to this potential type of terrorist attack. The cruise ship *Achille Lauro* was hijacked in October 1985, during which an American pensioner was murdered. The perpetrators then sank the ship and escaped on an Egyptian airliner.

Similar principles are used to assault trains and coaches, as both are capable of movement along a linear axis, i.e. a road or a rail line. Equally, they require stopping before any assault can be made. The SAS has worked on a number of assault methods, including dropping men from helicopters

Below: Freed hostages from the Depont train hijack in Holland, June 1977. The final assault on the train included a covert approach to the target and an excellent diversion (jet fighters).

onto trains and coaches. As both methods of transport are limited to speed and destination, the Anti-Terrorist Team can at least keep up with the hijacked transport, assaulting it when the opportunity arises.

Once stopped, both trains and coaches can be entered in a similar manner. Traditionally this is done by placing ladders against the vehicle and smashing in the windows and doors. As both means of transport are of fairly narrow dimensions, it is not always necessary to enter the vehicle in order to "pacify" any terrorists. If there is a need to enter, then stun grenades and CS gas will provide an excellent means of distraction.

The Depont train hijacking was one of the earliest instances of such vehicular terrorism. A train

travelling between Assen and Groningen in Holland was hijacked by nine Moluccan terrorists on 23 May 1977, with 51 hostages being taken. At the same time 110 hostages, mainly children, were seized at an elementary school at Bovensmilde, although 106 were released a few days later. The stand-off lasted for three weeks, until the psychiatrist who was conducting negotiations on behalf of the Dutch Government disclosed his concern that the terrorists were about to start killing the hostages. The Royal Dutch Marines Close-Combat Unit prepared to storm the train at 04:53

Below: Assaults against coaches are violent and overwhelming. The traditional method of entry is to place ladders against the vehicle and smash in the windows and doors.

hours, working in five-man teams. SAS advisors were in close contact throughout the hijack and recommended the use of stun grenades, but the Dutch decided against this, preferring instead to instigate the assault under the distraction of six F-104 Starfighters flying low over the train. In the ensuing assault six of the terrorists were killed and three surrendered. Two hostages, who panicked when the firing began, were also killed. One other hostage was also shot, albeit not fatally. In a simultaneous assault at the school the results were much better. Three of the four terrorists were caught unawares, asleep in their underwear, when the Marines broke through the school wall with an armoured vehicle. All four terrorists were captured and the hostages safely released.

CHAPTER 4

Surveillance Operations

Surveillance is not usually associated with SAS anti-terrorist operations, but collecting intelligence has long been the Regiment's business. This was especially true in Northern Ireland, where SAS soldiers spent hundreds of hours watching IRA suspects.

Rescuing hostages is just part of the anti-terrorist work carried out by the SAS. The SAS also plays a central role in surveillance operations. In the world of terrorism knowledge is everything; without it there is very little chance of successful operations. Although intelligence is obtained through a number of sources, the primary method is surveillance. As with any other aspect of anti-terrorist work, there are several working levels of surveillance, but the goal of all surveillance is intelligence. Intelligence is a safeguard against a nation's enemies, and consists of any information about a specific person, organization or country. The type of information can be anything and everything which has relevance to a security issue. Collected information is then processed, producing accurate intelligence, which in turn enables those in power to make a judgement on the appropriate action required.

Collecting intelligence involves human resources, such as those deployed by the Central Intelligence

Right: Many early SAS surveillance techniques were learned by lying in ditches or camouflaged in some underground hide. These simple methods often produce the best results.

Agency (CIA) in the US or Military Intelligence 5 (MI5) in Great Britain, while agencies such as the National Security Agency (NSA), Government Communications Headquarters (GCHQ), National Reconnaissance Office (NRO) and Joint Air Reconnaissance Centre (JARIC) rely on technological eavesdropping and satellite imagery. In addition to these agencies, international embassies normally have an operating system whereby information concerning the resident country is concentrated. There is also open information which is obtained largely by the world's media, in some cases a lot quicker than through government agencies.

Intelligence Assessments

One of the most important roles of intelligence personnel is to decide on the capability and intention of any suspects. The difference is important. Capability: "I know how to make a bomb from just about anything in the kitchen but I have no intention of doing so, because it's dangerous and illegal" (I have the capability but not the intention). Intention: "I don't know how to make a bomb but as soon as I am able I will kill my neighbour" (I do not have the ability but I have the intention to commit harm). Intelligence agencies are there to gather information about people who have both the capability and the intention. A perfect example is found in modern-day Iraq and its development of chemical and biological weapons: Saddam Hussein's regime has the capability and the intention for terrorism.

Who collects the information will depend largely on the enemy target and where that enemy is located. In most cases several agencies cooperate to achieve the same goal.

Individuals within terrorist groups use credit cards, mobile phones, vehicles, shipping or just walk down the street, and all these activities present surveillance opportunities. No matter

where they go they can be tracked. Even those rebels who live in remote areas can be found by the use of spy planes or satellite surveillance.

Where the SAS fits into this large picture of surveillance is hard to define, but it has always been an "information gatherer". In the days of the Cold War most British government departments were too busy spying on the former Soviet Union to bother with the situation developing in Northern Ireland. If SAS talents were required they would usually have been at the finishing end of a government operation, i.e. killing someone.

The SAS in Northern Ireland

For the most part any SAS surveillance in Northern Ireland was gathered to aid its own operations. Northern Ireland became the haven of the military intelligence officer. Consequently, once the SAS had been committed to Northern Ireland the "NI" Cell was set up.

This task was given to Captain Tony Ball who joined the SAS as a trooper, having initially joined the Parachute Regiment. He was commissioned and given the task of organizing the NI Cell that was to become the basis of the 14th Intelligence and Security Group. He did much to establish the undercover work carried out by the Regiment in Northern Ireland. Tony was an outstanding SAS officer with a brilliant future, but unfortunately he died in 1978 in a car accident.

Initial surveillance methods used by the SAS NI Cell were extremely primitive. The Cell mainly relied on converted cars, standard cameras and the "mark 1 eyeball" (a human being). Slowly new equipment started to arrive, mainly in the shape of excellent communications tools and improved photographic equipment. Although video was available at the time, it was in its infancy.

However, SAS communications improved dramatically thereafter, and around the late 1970s a

Above: Cars used for SAS surveillance operations may look ordinary, but they are in fact armour-plated, fitted with communications equipment and carrying firearms.

highly sophisticated spot-code system allowed a desk operator at base to plot the position of every vehicle moving around the Province. This system not only offered control during covert surveillance operations, but it also provided the Quick-Reaction Force (QRF) – British Army back-up – with a clear position should any SAS vehicle find itself in trouble.

A good example of this happened in Belfast, when a car belonging to the 14th Intelligence and Security Group (know as the "Detachment") found itself being pursued by four Irish Republican Army (IRA) gunmen. The undercover operator radioed in

giving his location using the spot-code and help was dispatched. Unfortunately, before help could arrive the IRA car sped past the undercover agent and screeched to a halt. The operator later told me the story in his own words. "I just knew that I had been tumbled [exposed] and that the four men in the car behind me were about to stitch me. I radioed for back-up but a few seconds later the car overtook me and braked hard, forcing me to stop against the curb. I had an M10 machine pistol under my seat which was ready to go, however I decided to put my trust in the Browning 9mm in my waist holster. The door of my car was armoured, so I got out using it as a shield. I was already on my feet as the first IRA member opened the driver's side rear door. The guy was having

trouble bringing his rifle to bear, so I shot him from a distance of about three metres. The next head to appear was from the front passenger seat, he also had a rifle. I shot him in the head. It then dawned on me that these idiots were using weapons [all had rifles which are difficult to manoeuvre when exiting a car] not compatible with this type of ambush. I shot the third terrorist just as he turned. I then casually walked up to the driver and shot him."

Although being early in the morning the gunfire had brought many people onto the street, but when they saw the dead bodies they soon disappeared. Shortly after back-up arrived.

One of the most ingenious surveillance operations started in the early days of the "troubles" in Northern Ireland. Who actually came up with the idea I have never been able to discover. The operation involved the setting up of a company called Four Square Laundry. This in fact was a front for a British military entity known as the Military

Reconnaissance Force (MRF), one of the first undercover units to function in Northern Ireland during the early 1970s. One of its tasks was to operate a mobile laundry service collecting from house to house, mainly in the poorer Catholic areas. It was assured of good custom, as its prices were far lower than its nearest rivals. Prior to washing, all the clothes would pass through a special forensic test, which checked for explosives. Traces found would indicate where bombs were being assembled and also provide an address. Unfortunately, several members of the MRF who had been former members of the IRA converted to work for the British changed back their allegiance. This led to a Four Square van being shot up; the male driver was killed but the woman passenger managed to escape.

One problem did exist for which there seemed no answer. Despite the professionalism of the SAS and the Detachment it was, and still is, difficult for those who were born and raised in mainland Britain to pass themselves off as being from Northern Ireland. Certain surveillance tasks require operators to have the ability to mix and talk with locals. A few SAS, especially those who had been born in Ireland, were able to achieve this, but by and large "Brits" trying to pass themselves off as Irishmen were easily spotted. A perfect example of this resulted in the death of Captain Robert Nairac. Nairac was attached to the 14th Intelligence and Security Group and was killed by the IRA in May 1977. At the time he was working with the SAS detachment located at Bessbrook, South Armagh. A highly intelligent officer, Nairac had been educated at Ampleforth Catholic School, before attending Lincoln College, Oxford, where he read history. After Sandhurst he joined the Grenadier Guards, before being transferred to the Detachment.

Captain Robert Nairac

Nairac perfected an Irish accent and made a detailed study of the local customs and Republican protocol. He purchased Republican song sheets, which he learnt and would sing in the public houses along the border with Eire.

On one such evening, while visiting the *Three Steps Inn* at Drumintee, some 4.8km (three miles) from the border, he sang several songs to a packed house. He went to leave around 23:30 hours and headed for the car park. At his car he was confronted by a number of men curious as to his identification. A fight ensued (Nairac was an

excellent boxer), and during the scuffle his 9mm Browning pistol fell to the ground, giving away his identity. He was soon overpowered. Blindfolded and gagged, Nairac was taken first to a house where he tried in vain to escape, after which he was moved by car to a field whereupon he was tortured. Despite being beaten repeatedly to the ground with a fence post, Captain Nairac refused to talk. In the end he was shot with his own pistol and his body disposed of, never to be recovered. Some years after his death, information from an eyewitness verified the punishment Nairac had suffered, and the IRA grudgingly applauded the man's courage. His body was never found, and it was widely rumoured that his remains had been converted to animal feed.

I was with Bob Nairac the day before he was captured. We had spent the day in Belfast purchasing several song sheets. I was also present in Gough Barracks (Special Branch HQ for the South) when a man under interrogation confessed to being a witness to the final demise of Captain Nairac.

To some degree, this problem of finding convincing undercover operators was overcome when a unit of the Royal Ulster Constabulary (RUC) in Northern Ireland was established that specialized in surveillance and the gathering of

Right: *SAS soldiers on surveillance operations always carry weapons for back-up. The most popular firearm is the Browning Hi-Power pistol. Browning products are extremely reliable.*

Above: Captain Robert Nairac GC was an excellent SAS under-cover operator who paid the ultimate price for working alone and not having back-up. He was brutally murdered by the IRA.

intelligence. The unit, known as E4A, underwent its initial training with the SAS at Hereford. The unit became fully operational in 1978. As E4A proved its worth, it took over much of the work previously undertaken by the 14th Intelligence and Security Group. Surveillance by E4A provided excellent information such as on the attack on the RUC station at Loughall (see Chapter 6).

The SAS surveillance role in Northern Ireland continued to grow, helping develop both tactics and equipment. Camera systems became more advanced, and the larger SAS cells operating in the Province had their own photographic studios, which helped not only with speed of processing but also with security. Infrared film and flash adaptors were also widely used, allowing the Close Target

Reconnaissance (CTR) teams to make a visual record of their night's investigations without drawing attention to themselves. Long-range photographic lenses were also used, allowing good quality photographs even at distances of over 1000m (3048ft). Large-scale photographs for operational planning came from RAF surveillance aircraft flying from Aldergrove airport (by the late 1970s there was excellent coverage available of almost every part of Northern Ireland). If a more detailed aerial view was required then a flyover could be arranged within a few hours.

Surveillance Techniques

Both static and mobile observation vehicles form an important part of any surveillance operation. They can be manned or unmanned depending on the requirements. As a rule, the larger the vehicle the more suspicion it draws. For example, a large delivery van is more prominent than a standard car. A good walk-past of the location should reveal the type of vehicle best suited for the surveillance operation. Parking directly across the street is a bit obvious, added to which access to a parking space is not always guaranteed. Surveillance operators learn a lot of tricks when it comes to watching their target. Placing a video or fixed camera is easy, it's making sure the device is not discovered which requires the skill. Many terrorists will have received some form of anti-surveillance training. If a strange vehicle turns up opposite their home for more than a few hours, they may become suspicious. One tried and tested method for those who think they are under surveillance is to approach the vehicle and bang on the doors or, if not obscured, look through every window. This has the effect of making the surveillance unit think they've been spotted and replace the vehicle. Today we know this would be wrong. The sudden disappearance of the vehicle would only confirm the target's suspicions. A good surveillance unit would hold firm, trusting that any camera had been hidden well enough to avoid even the closest scrutiny.

One of the best surveillance operations I was involved with in Northern Ireland required that we should enter a certain house in a street. The house was occupied most of the time, making entry into the building difficult. Finally we entered the house by removing the back door of a bank in the same street. The door and its frame were removed while the alarm system was still operating. Once inside the bank, we gained access to the roof and removed enough bricks to allow us to make our way to the target house. A covert camera was installed, with the power supply being taken from the lighting circuit. As a result of this surveillance, three men who were on their

way to assassinate a district judge were arrested with their weapons.

Surveillance information can be acquired from a number of sources, but for SAS operations they are normally restricted to vehicular and static observation. Vehicular surveillance normally requires a target to be followed around by a set of covert cars. The techniques used have been refined down to a fine art. The object of the surveillance is to find out where the target vehicle is going, and if possible who the occupants meet. The added use of a surveillance helicopter means that the cars can fall back in order to avoid being detected by the target. This system, while offering excellent monitoring of the target, had its drawbacks. Cost, both in money and manpower, was often excessive, added to which it was highly possible that the target would spot the vehicles or helicopter and so terminate any activity that would get him or her arrested. The advent of tracking devices in 1988 has diminished this more traditional surveillance method, making

Below: *Crossmaglen, near the Irish border, was an Ulster town noted for high IRA activity. It was therefore the scene of intensive SAS surveillance operations.*

it possible for one operator to follow several vehicles at once.

When it comes to static surveillance they say that SAS soldiers can hide anywhere. This is partly true. In the past I have seen men bury themselves by constructing a hide in a graveyard. Such hides were very uncomfortable and, I am glad to say, for the most part they are a thing of the past. Likewise, the use of manned, static surveillance vehicles has diminished. Most have been replaced by video cameras and whisper microphones hidden in inanimate objects. However, the SAS will still use manned vehicles if it feels the target has bomb-making equipment or weapons in the location. The sudden removal of these could indicate an imminent attack. In either case, the first step in any surveillance operation is to carry out a CTR.

A CTR is designed to establish the basic fundamentals of the target location, i.e. what the building looks like; how is the immediate area populated; how many people, if any, live in the same building; are there any dogs; and does the target have a car? In some cases CTRs are done to establish the presence of incriminating evidence, weapons or bomb-making material. A good CTR will also establish how difficult the target will be to observe on a day-to-day basis.

Newry

A typical surveillance operation in which I was involved took part in Newry, Northern Ireland. Newry town hall sits across a river, an area known locally as Sugar Island. It came to prominence with the SAS when it was tasked by British Special Branch police to observe a suspected IRA member who went by the name of "Teasy Weasy MacDonald", owing to the fact that he was a hairdresser. His shop was situated on the second-floor corner of a building very close to Sugar Island, and after several CTRs the only building

Above: *A picture of the author taken in the late 1970s in the Special Branch office in Dungannon, Northern Ireland. The SAS made great use of cameras during surveillance missions.*

found suitable to serve as an observation point was the town hall. Special Branch was approached to confirm access but declined on account of security. Nevertheless, further CTRs carried out by the SAS were unable to find any other location that would allow observation through the second-floor windows of the hairdresser. It was decided to use the town hall and not inform Special Branch.

Climbers from Mountain Troop literally scaled an outside wall some 23m (70ft) high and aided the establishment of a two-man observation team onto the roof. It was discovered that there existed a small space between the outside roof and a decorated plaster inner roof. Part of this inner roof had a

Above: Surveillance in Sugar Island, Newry. A rare picture taken inside a small hide the SAS established behind the town hall clock. The photograph was taken using infrared flash and film.

platform with a small access door in order to service the town-hall clock. This platform, which was little more than 2 x 1m (6 x 3ft), allowed the two SAS operators to remain undetected for several weeks. On either side of the clock face, which was permanently illuminated by eight light bulbs, there were sets of slats which acted as air vents. The left-hand vent looked down into the hairdresser's window, allowing photographs to be taken of all visitors to the shop. Two SAS operators stayed in this position for almost three weeks.

Because the town hall was occupied most of the time, no cooking was allowed and the two men lived on cold sandwiches and hot drinks delivered

in thermos flasks by the support team. The support team would also take away body waste and litter, together with any reports and film taken by the observation post. This precaution of removing everything meant that the two men could escape if discovered without leaving evidence behind. While the surveillance produced no firm evidence of the hairdresser being involved in IRA activity, it did indicate that a known IRA man was having an illicit affair with the wife of another IRA man who was currently serving 10 years in prison. This information was later used in a "sting" operation and both the man and adulterous wife were "persuaded" to work for the security forces.

Today, hidden video cameras and microphones would cover the same situation. Yet while these provide excellent visual and audio documentation, they lack the ability to interpret a series of actions that lead to a conclusion, such as the case above where adultery was revealed. The "mark 1 eyeball" and a human brain will always be central to effective surveillance.

Coalisland Shooting

On Sunday 4 December 1983, an SAS OP (Observation Position) which had been watching an IRA arms cache, opened fire on two men who arrived to collect weapons with the intention of committing a murder. The weapons were housed in a hide protected by a thick hedgerow that separated a small field from a quiet country lane. A gateway into the field provided easy access. Once the hide was discovered a full-scale operation was mounted. This involved 14th Intelligence and Surveillance Group, which was responsible for watching the IRA suspects. The SAS would provide cover and E4A would form a Quick-Reaction Force (QRF). The SAS inserted several two-man OPs around the field, with the main OP in a ditch opposite the weapons hide, some 20m (61ft) away. E4A were positioned at

Lurgan, while "14 Int" carried out tight surveillance. The SAS men in the OPs remained in position despite the wet and cold December weather. Around 15:15 hours on Sunday afternoon, a car was heard slowing and it eventually stopped opposite the gate. Two men got out and climbed the gate, leaving the driver in the car. They walked directly to the hide, knelt down and retrieved the weapons.

A Clean, Neat Job

The first terrorist, Colm McGirr, pulled out a weapon and passed it to the second, Brian Campbell. As Campbell stood, turning back in the direction of the car, the two SAS men challenged him from the OP. McGirr, who was still kneeling by the bush, turned with a gun in his hand and was shot dead. Campbell ran for the gate still holding the weapon. Two more shots rang out and he fell mortally wounded. The driver, on hearing the gunfire and realizing that it was a trap, drove off. An SAS soldier jumped out to stop him, firing four high-velocity rounds directly into the car but failing to hit him. A quick check indicated that McGirr was dead, but Campbell was still breathing and an SAS medic inserted an airway and administered first aid; Campbell died before the ambulance crew arrived some 20 minutes later.

The area was sealed off by E4A, who were activated via radio instructions to search for the missing get-away car. It was quickly located near some houses about a mile away. Despite a great deal of blood in the car, the injured driver was not to be found. It was later learned that he had been whisked away by local Republican sympathizers, who managed to get him across the border into the Irish Republic before any road-blocks could be set up. In the eyes of the SAS it was a clean, neat job, apart from preventing the vehicle to get away, for which the SAS soldier concerned was severely criticized by the "head-shed" (SAS headquarters at Hereford).

Above: *Often the "mark 1 eyeball" surveillance technique is the best for getting accurate information. A single SAS soldier lying in a hole can achieve excellent results.*

Surveillance operations continue in Northern Ireland, as they do wherever Great Britain has interests. Despite the fact that the trail (as I write this)

for Osama bin Laden has gone cold, the worldwide net around terrorism is tightening and the keepers of this net are the surveillance units around the world. Recently, all eyes have turned to shipping, as intelligence services around the world search for at least 20 ships thought to make up a terrorist fleet linked to Osama bin Laden's *Al Qaeda* group.

Tracking ships and boarding them is a logistical nightmare hampered by the controversial "flags of convenience" system, under which many ships are registered as Panamanian, Liberian or Cypriot to avoid stringent checks on their crews and cargoes. To help ease the problem, the American ports authority now insist on 96 hours' notice before any

Above: Surveillance operations in Northern Ireland always have armed reinforcements close by to protect SAS teams. Most terrorists will try to fight their way out of an ambush.

Most of this is closing the door after the horse has bolted, and I find myself asking the question: where was our surveillance leading up to 11 September 2001? If we are to believe that Osama bin Laden was hiding in Afghanistan at the time, how come we didn't pick up any communications or couriers between there and America? There had to be some – the operation against America was carried out only after the perpetrators had undergone serious long-term training. To get the timing right someone must have been coordinating the attack. How come we missed it all? Personally I can't help feeling that we have forsaken the "mark 1 eyeball" for too much technology. Don't get me wrong, technology is very good, but most of it fails when it comes to interpretation of information. Most modern surveillance operators are desk-bound and have very little field experience. What is needed is more know-how that builds up over the years and provides a "gut feeling" for trouble. It is this mixture of combat and covert operations which makes the SAS so aptly suited to surveillance.

Harnessing Technology

That is not to say that the SAS ignores technology; on the contrary, if it helps win the fight the Regiment will embrace it. We must put things in perspective, though. We have all seen movies where the good guys are following the bad guys around using a sophisticated set of spy satellites and a laptop computer. The surveillance satellites are good and getting better, but so far the resolution is still not good enough to identify and track individuals walking around the streets, never mind spy on them while they go underground or indoors. Trust me, it will be some years before "big brother" has you under visual observation directly from a satellite in the way the movies portray it.

That said, it is possible to track both an individual or a vehicle using satellite technology, in

ship docks and a full list of the crew in advance. Since the attack in 2001 on the American destroyer USS *Cole*, naval ships are now requesting a 450m (1371ft) exclusion zone around their vessels. This means that any ship, even while in dock, must not approach a warship. If circumstances demand (i.e. in a narrow dock) that another vessel has to pass within 450m (1371ft), then it must radio the warship for permission. While this is a good precaution, the ship that smashed a hole in the side of USS *Cole* was a Rigid Inflatable Boat (RIB) that had been packed with explosives. With the right engine, an RIB can cover 450m (1371ft) in less that 30 seconds.

Above: The American Predator unmanned aerial vehicle is used for surveillance. Flying at high altitudes, it can relay "real time" intelligence to operatives on the ground.

fact it's fairly simple. You can even buy a system yourself for around $500 or less on the internet. The two main elements in this system are the satellites which deliver the Global Positioning System (GPS) coordinates, and the Global System for Mobiles telephone network. Groupe Spécial Mobile (GSM) was developed in the early 1980s. Analogue cellular telephone systems were experiencing rapid growth in Europe, particularly in Scandinavia and Great Britain, but also in France and West Germany. Each country developed its own system, which was incompatible with everyone else's equipment and operation. This was an undesirable situation, because not only was the mobile equipment limited to operation within national boundaries, which in a unified Europe were increasingly irrelevant, but there was a very limited market for each type of equipment. This situation could not continue.

In 1982 the Conference of European Posts and Telegraphs (CEPT) formed the GSM to study and develop a pan-European public land-mobile system. A commercial service was started in mid-1991, and by 1993 there were 36 GSM networks in 22 countries, with 25 additional countries having already selected or considering GSM. The European GSM standard was also accepted by South Africa, Australia and most of the Middle and Far East. The initials GSM now stand for Global System for Mobile telecommunications.

Developed by the United State's Department of Defense, the GPS system consists of 24 military satellites that orbit the earth continually, giving out the time and their position. Receiver units on earth pick up this information and convert it into precise coordinates of their locations. Designed primarily for the military, the GPS system now guides most of the world's shipping, aircraft and smart bombs. The receiver unit can be quite small; one can even be fitted into a wristwatch. The GPS receiver unit searches for and then locks onto any satellite signals. The more signals you receive the greater the accuracy, but a minimum of four is sufficient. The information received is then collated into a usable form; for example, a grid reference, height above sea

Below: This is a leaflet distributed by the Americans following the 11 September 2001 attack against New York – proof that surveillance technology and methods can fail.

level, or a longitude and latitude. By measuring your position in relation to a number of known objects, i.e. the satellites, the receiver is able to calculate your exact position. This is called satellite ranging. It is also able to update your position and speed and track you while you are on the move. Devices can be attached to both people and vehicles, which receive the GPS signal and transmit it to a laptop computer via the GSM network. Providing you have digital mapping of the area, the signal can be synchronized to coincide with a visual ground map. Several tracking devices, which are no larger than cigarette packs, can be used at the same time, all with individual identification tags.

GPS is global, but where the GSM signal is not available the tracking signal is stored by the device

until the person or vehicle being tracked comes under the GSM signal once more. In the event this does not happen, the device can be removed and analyzed to reveal where the person or vehicle went while out of GSM range.

There are items other than GPS trackers which are used in surveillance. For example, a whisper microphone or video can be covertly fitted inside a car, which in turn will transmit a signal to the tracking device (normally attached by magnet under the vehicle). This allows the surveillance personnel, who may be using a laptop in Malaysia, both to see and listen to the conversation of a person being tracked in America. If time permits their fitting, there are other pieces of technology which will allow an operator to interfere with the vehicle, speed it up, slow it down and even lock the doors. Where people are about to commit a terrorist action, a small pre-planted explosive device can be detonated inside the car.

The military have been using infrared and thermal-imaging devices on the battlefield since the early 1970s, and like most equipment they have evolved rapidly. Infrared (IR) energy is electromagnetic radiation that travels in a straight line through space, similar to visible light. The term infrared refers to the frequency of the electromagnetic energy, which is "infra" or "below" the red range of the visible spectrum. As the frequency of the electromagnetic energy increases, the length of the waves decreases. Infrared shares many of the properties of visible light, but its

BACK

PUSHTO		DARI
UP TO A $25,000,000 REWARD FOR INFORMATION LEADING TO THE WHEREABOUTS OR CAPTURE OF THESE TWO MEN.	USAMA BIN LADEN AIMAN AL-ZAWAHIRI	UP TO A $25,000,000 REWARD FOR INFORMATION LEADING TO THE WHEREABOUTS OR CAPTURE OF THESE TWO MEN.

different wavelength has several unique characteristics. For instance, materials that are opaque to visible light may be transparent to infrared, and vice versa. Infrared is less subject to scattering and absorption by smoke or dust than visible light, and cannot be seen by the human eye. Also, unlike visible light, which is given off by ordinary objects only at very high temperatures, infrared is emitted by all objects at ordinary temperatures. This means infrared is all around us all the time, even in the dark. Different objects give off varying amounts of infrared, depending on the temperature of the object and also on a characteristic called "emissivity". Infrared torches and searchlights are also manufactured, and while these are not visible to the human eye, used with the right type of scope they work just like a normal torch.

Night Vision

Low-light image intensifiers electronically increase the amount of light available at night, even that emitted by the stars. Such devices have been developed into a number of applications. Military pilots fly their aircraft and deliver their payloads in total darkness using passive night goggles (PNGs). A similar technology is used by the SAS for carrying out night-time CTRs. The lens on a camera or video allows for covert night filming. Gone are the days when you could hide in the dark – infrared, image intensifiers or thermal vision will find you. In addition to seeing the enemy, we can also listen to his conversation.

Both land-line and mobile-phone monitoring are highly advanced. It is now possible to listen and record most conversations between two people, and you don't even have to be in the same country. Email and faxes can be interrupted, have the wording changed and you would never know. Video cameras and associated accessories have also

become more sophisticated. It is now possible to secrete a camera no bigger than a pin head into most items: pens, clocks, ties or toys. Many such cameras have a built-in transmitter capable of sending the pictures to a remote monitor or recorder. Like any other well organized anti-terrorist unit, the SAS has access to a myriad of surveillance devices. Unfortunately, most of this kit is also available to the terrorist. Walk into any high-street electronic store and you will find thermal-image devices, watch cameras and so on. Specialist equipment is easily available over the Internet, another system terrorists use to advance their cause.

Right: Members of the SAS Anti-Terrorist Team are equipped with the latest night-vision devices to enable them to see in buildings where there is low light.

Above: The Global Positioning System (GPS) provides 24-hour and three-dimensional (latitude, longitude and altitude) positioning to any user anywhere in the world.

CHAPTER 5

Foreign Assignments

The SAS's expertise in counter-terrorism has resulted in its men being sent all over the world to advise foreign governments. In addition, its soldiers have also been sent abroad by the British Government to defend British interests and those of its allies.

The SAS Anti-Terrorist Team has carried out several major operations abroad. Some of these have been as a direct result of Irish Republican Army (IRA) overseas activities, or at the request of a foreign government.

In certain circumstances the British Government may deem it necessary to commit the SAS into another country in order to preserve that country's democracy or to fight tyranny.

A perfect example of cooperation happened in October 1977 when the West German Chancellor Herr Schmidt called British Prime Minister James Callaghan. Chancellor Schmidt opened the conversation with remarks about the current situation regarding the hijack of Lufthansa flight LH181. At this stage, he had been informed of a British specialist group known as the SAS, of whom everyone seemed to hold a very high opinion. He was particularly interested in its specialist knowledge of the Middle East and the new weaponry in its arsenal. As the prime minister

Left: Peruvian police take up defensive positions outside the Japanese Embassy in Lima following the terrorist attack, 27 January 1997. The SAS was called in to assist the Peruvians.

listened, Chancellor Schmidt proposed such specialist knowledge could be extremely useful in bringing the hijack to a peaceful end. He then indicated, in confidence, that West Germany was considering making an assault on the aircraft and he asked whether the SAS could help. As a direct result the prime minister sent myself and Alastair Morrison to assist the Germans.

A Coup in The Gambia

Another excellent example of SAS foreign operations took place in August 1981, when Margaret Thatcher dispatched two SAS men to The Gambia. It had been a busy time for the Regiment, which had been drafted in to help with the protection of numerous VIPs. A large number of Commonwealth heads of state had been in London attending the wedding of Prince Charles to Lady Diana Spencer. The gathering of notables presented a number of opportunities for terrorists. It was then that Major Ian Crooke, who was acting Executive Officer of the Regiment at the time, learned that the small nation of The Gambia, a former British colony, was in the throes of a coup d'etat. Launched two days earlier, it coincided with the absence of the nation's president, Sir Dawda Jawara, who was representing his country at the royal wedding. Senegal, The Gambia's neighbour, who had a military agreement for just such an emergency, had already sent troops to combat the rebels. Additionally, Jawara had asked the prime minister for help, and she agreed to dispatch a couple of SAS men to the scene. Crooke chose one other SAS man, selected whatever weapons and equipment he would need, and caught the next available aircraft to Senegal.

The revolt was organized by the Gambian Socialist Revolutionary Party, which was headed by a young Marxist named Kukoi Samba Sanyang. His given name was Dominique. When he became a communist, he changed it to Kukoi, a word in the

Above: *Libyan leader Colonel Muammar Gaddafi provided aid to the Gambian rebels in 1981. He has supported anti-imperialist and Arab nationalist groups since the early 1970s.*

Mandinka language native to The Gambia that means "sweep clean". Sanyang was also among the African radicals who had sojourned in Libya. The volatile Libyan leader Colonel Gaddafi envisioned a confederation of Islamic African states under his guidance. At 05:00 hours on Thursday 30 July 1981, the coup erupted. Muscle for the attempt to overthrow Jawara was provided by Usman Bojang, a former deputy commander of The Gambia's 300-man Police Field Force, a paramilitary organization charged with preserving order in the tiny country. Bojang managed to persuade or force the contingent based in the town of Bakau to join the coup. This group, which amounted to about one-third of the organization, disarmed most of the loyal police, then quickly took over the nearby transmitter for Radio Gambia and moved into Banjul, the capital. On the way they opened the country's largest prison and distributed weapons from the police armoury, not only to the inmates but to virtually anyone who happened along. Not long after daybreak, citizens and former prisoners alike began rampaging through the streets and looting shops. Soon, a free-for-all erupted.

"Dictatorship of the Proletariat"

Within the first few hours of the coup, scores of bodies – policemen, criminals and civilians – littered the streets of Banjul. Arriving at Radio Gambia shortly after, rebel policemen seized the station and Sanyang closed the country's borders and its airport at Yundum, some 24km (15 miles) east of Banjul. Then he proclaimed a "dictatorship of the proletariat" and charged the "bourgeois" Jawara government with corruption, injustice and nepotism. Most Europeans and Americans working in business or holding government posts kept off the streets. While other foreigners and tourists stayed in the capital, or remained in their hotels in the nearby communities of Bakau and Fajara, many rebel Gambian policemen, who saw no profit in harming Western individuals, guided anxious foreigners to the residence of the United States ambassador, Larry G. Piper. The house was soon a haven to 123 nervous guests, 80 of them American

citizens. A number of European tourists also sought shelter in the Atlantic Beach Hotel, on the outskirts of Banjul, along the nation's beautiful sea coast.

During the trouble, two armed looters raided the hotel, ransacked the safe and took the local manager hostage. As they fled the hotel, gunshots were heard and the two looters were shot dead in the hotel doorway. Fearing more looters would arrive and hearing the constant firing outside, the hotel guests organized watches and posted guards "armed" with fire extinguishers. Around this time, Ian Crooke and an SAS sergeant, Tony (not his real name), had chosen and assembled all their weapons and equipment. These consisted of German-made Heckler & Koch submachine guns, Browning 9mm semi-automatic pistols, and a stock of ammunition and grenades. Crooke managed to pass his little arsenal through customs and baggage checks and onto the first flight available. Informal contacts within the British diplomatic service cleared the way in minutes. As always, Ian and Tony were dressed in casual attire, prompting no attention from their fellow passengers, amongst whom were many reporters and television camera crews.

The SAS Team Arrives in The Gambia

Upon arriving in Senegal, Ian Crooke encountered his first obstacle: British diplomats. Despite the brief from the prime minister directly to the SAS, the diplomats refused to allow them to get involved. Undeterred, Ian Crooke decided to go ahead with his mission despite the remonstrations of these relatively minor officials. Adopting the policy of out of sight, out of mind, the two men managed to get seats on a plane bound for The Gambia's Yundum airport. Upon arrival he met up with the Senegalese paratroop commander, Lieutenant-Colonel Abdourah-man N'Gom, who had established his headquarters in the confines of the airport. For the Senegalese troops capturing

Yundum airport had not been easy. During a fierce battle almost half the 120 paratroops making the assault were wounded or killed. Once this task was completed, Senegalese soldiers entered Banjul and within a few hours they had cleared it of rebels.

Shortly after the SAS arrived they met up with Clive Lee, a hulking 1.98m- (6ft 6in-) tall retired SAS major who was employed as a civilian adviser to the Gambian Pioneer Corps, a division of the Field Force that trained rural youth in agricultural and construction skills. Hearing of the coup on the radio, Lee had rounded up 23 Pioneer Corps members, armed them, and set off for Banjul (you can't keep a good SAS man down when he smells a fight). To get there from the Pioneer Corps base in the town of Farafenni, 96.6km (60 miles) east of the capital, Lee had to cross the Gambia River. Because of the hostilities, however, the ferry had suspended operations. As with Ian Crooke and the diplomats, this was no time for gentlemanly actions, and soon the ferry captain had been "persuaded" to take Lee's band to the other side. Once in Banjul Lee's party made for police headquarters, where it reinforced a small contingent of loyalists and set about defending its enclave by barricading nearby streets.

Military Stalemate

The Senegalese continued to strengthen their forces in The Gambia, but soon the military situation had reached an impasse. Senegalese troops were stalled outside Bakau because the rebels had taken more than 100 hostages. The most valuable captives were Lady Chilel N'Jie – one of President Jawara's two wives – and a number of his children. In addition, they held several members of the Gambian cabinet. Furthermore, although the Senegalese had wrested Radio Gambia from Sanyang's rebels (the transmitter lay between the airport and the bridge), the coup leader had commandeered a mobile

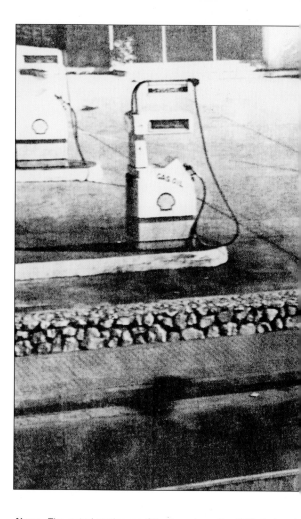

Above: The petrol station on Gibraltar where the SAS shot and killed the IRA terrorists in March 1988. The terrorists had made movements that suggested they were reaching for weapons.

transmitter from which Lady Chilel appealed almost hysterically to Senegal, announcing that the hostages would be executed unless the paratroops withdrew. Sanyang repeated the threat himself. "I shall kill the whole lot," he warned, "and thereafter stand to fight the Senegalese."

On 5 August, Crooke decided to make a reconnaissance. The blue-jeans-clad SAS officer and his two associates slipped forward of Senegalese outposts and set out on foot. Crooke's sortie confirmed that the insurgents were now capable of little more than token resistance

There was sporadic violent gunfire," said Felon, "then the two men walked calmly back to our hotel."

Arriving at the British High Commissioner's offices, Crooke learned that armed rebel guards had escorted President Jawara's wife and her four ailing children – one of them an infant of only five weeks – to a British clinic the day before. This information came by way of a telephone call to the High Commissioner from the British physician attending the children. In return, the official told the doctor that armed SAS men would be there within minutes, and Crooke and his two companions quickly headed for the hospital. As Crooke approached the hospital, he noticed two armed guards posted at the entrance. Handing his submachine gun to his companions, the major gave them the order to circle behind the guards, then walked up to the pair and distracted them in conversation as the other two SAS men crept up from the rear. Crooke's ruse worked and the two guards froze when they felt gun muzzles at the back of their heads.

The End of the Coup

Crooke slipped inside the clinic where he surprised Lady Chilel's weaponless escorts as they watched the children being treated and promptly took them prisoner. After conducting the President's wife and children to the High Commissioner's office, Crooke and his party retreated to N'Gom's headquarters at the airport. A day earlier, Senegalese troops, who now numbered about 1500, had found and destroyed the mobile transmitter being used by the rebels. With the silencing of its leaders, the coup's backbone was broken. Yet many hostages remained under rebel guns at a police barracks, and disorganized bands of turncoat policemen and criminals had to be rounded up. Eight days later the rebellion was all over, but it had caused over 1000 deaths. President Jawara was once again the

against well-trained Senegalese troops. For this reason, Crooke persuaded N'Gom to begin an advance on Fajara and Bakau the same day. The British officer and his companions accompanied a contingent of Senegalese troops along the hot byways of the suburbs. Peter Felon, a British engineer employed by an American crane company, saw the party when they appeared at his hotel in Fajara. "Ten Senegalese troops and a British Army officer arrived at the hotel," the engineer recalled. The officer, probably Clive Lee, wore khakis with no insignia. "With him were two men who I can only describe as the most vicious-looking professionals I have ever seen. Upon being told that rebels were hiding along a creek near the beach, the pair set off to find them.

Above: Peruvian special forces storm the Japanese Embassy in Lima in April 1997. SAS specialists were sent to Peru by the British Government to advise on an assault.

unchallenged and elected head of the Gambian government. Kukoi Sanyang was eventually arrested in the neighbouring country of Guinea-Bissau, but the socialist government there later released him, despite Gambian requests for his extradition.

Senegalese troops captured more than 100 of the rebels and convicts, seven of whom were ultimately condemned to death. Libya was never connected directly with the coup attempt. The SAS men hung around The Gambia just long enough to satisfy themselves that British citizens would be safe.

The operation in The Gambia demonstrated how a few skilled and confident soldiers can influence an event far out of proportion to their numbers.

Above: The three IRA terrorists who were prevented by the SAS from committing an atrocity in Gibraltar: Sean Savage (left), Mairead Farrell (centre) and Danny McCann (right).

Additionally, they could disappear as if nothing had happened, adding yet more mystique to the SAS myth.

Counter-IRA Operations

As mentioned earlier, some foreign operations have been in reaction to IRA activities abroad. The famous incident in Gibraltar in 1988 is a good illustration. In late 1987, a well-known IRA bomb-maker, Sean Savage, had been located in Spain. With him was Daniel McCann, another IRA suspect. MI5 spent the next six months watching the two, gathering vital information that they were certain was leading to a bombing. When, on 4 March 1988, Mairead Farrell, another IRA operative, arrived at Malaga Airport and was met by the two men, it seemed likely that the bombing was on. At this stage the SAS was invited to send in a team. The Gibraltar police were informed of the operation, and instructed that the IRA active service

unit was to be apprehended. For a while, contact with the IRA cell was lost, but by this time the target had been defined. It was suspected that one car would be driven onto the Rock, and parked in a position along the route taken by the military parade. This car would be clean, a dummy to guarantee a parking space for the real car bomb. The best spot to cause the most damage was thought to be the Plaza, where British troops conducted regular ceremonies and the public would assemble to watch. This proved to be correct.

At 14:00 hours on 5 March, a report was received that Savage had been spotted in a parked white Renault 5. There was a suspicion that he was setting up the bomb-triggering device. Not long after, another report was received to the effect that Farrell and McCann had crossed the border into Gibraltar and were making their way into town. Gonzo (nickname of the SAS field commander) and his guys were immediately deployed, and once Savage was out of the way an explosives expert did a walk past of the Renault. No visual tell-tale signs were observed, such as the rear suspension being depressed, indicating the presence of a bomb. However, if they were using Semtex, 14kg (30lb) or more could be easily concealed to the naked eye. After consultation, it was considered probable that the car did contain a bomb. At this stage the local police chief, Joseph Canepa, signed an order passing control to the SAS. Operation Flavius, as it was known, was about to be concluded. The orders stated that the SAS were to capture the three bombers if possible. But as in all such situations, if there is a direct threat to life, be it to the SAS or anyone else, they had the right to shoot. It was stressed that the bomb would more than likely be fired on a push-button detonator. So, dressed in casual clothes and keeping in contact through small radios hidden about their person, the SAS soldiers shadowed the terrorist. Each SAS member was armed with a 9mm Browning Hi-Power pistol.

Gun Battle in Gibraltar

Savage met up with McCann and Farrell, and after a short discussion all three made their way back towards the Spanish border. Four SAS men continued to shadow the trio. Suddenly, for some unexplained reason, Savage turned around and started to make his way back into the town. The SAS guys split; two with Savage; two staying on McCann and Farrell. A few moments later, fate took a hand. A local policeman, driving in heavy traffic, was recalled to the station. It was said later that to expedite his orders he activated his siren. This action happened close to McCann and Farrell, making the pair turn nervously. McCann made eye contact with one of the SAS men, who was no more than 10m (30ft) away. In response to this, the SAS were about to issue a challenge when McCann's arm moved distinctly across his body. Fearing that he may detonate the bomb, the SAS drew their weapons and fired. McCann was hit just below the nose, snapping his head back; a second shot took

him through the throat. Farrell made a movement for her bag. Again fearing she was going for a gun or presser switch, the SAS soldiers fired. She was shot with a single round. On hearing the shots Savage had turned, only to be confronted by the other two SAS men. A warning was shouted this time, but Savage continued to reach into his pocket – both soldiers fired and Savage was killed.

Media Frenzy

As the first news of the event hit the media, it looked like a professional job, but the euphoria was short-lived. No bomb was found in the car, and all three terrorists were found to be unarmed. Although a bomb was later discovered in Malaga, the press and the IRA had a field day. Allegations were made and witnesses were found who claimed to have seen the whole thing. The trio had surrendered; their arms had been in the air; they had been shot at point-blank range while they lay on the ground, and so on. Once again the SAS men were held up as killers. No matter that they had probably saved the lives of many people, and dispatched three well-known IRA terrorists. The guys returned to the UK and were put through the mill – eventually they would stand trial. In September 1988, after a two-week inquest and by a majority of nine to two, a verdict was passed of lawful killing. Although this satisfied most people, the story did not end there. The SAS soldiers who took part in the shooting in Gibraltar were taken to court by relatives of the three IRA members killed. The European Commission in Strasbourg decided 11 to 6 that the SAS did not use unnecessary force. They said that the soldiers were justified in opening fire as the IRA members were about to detonate a bomb. However, they did refer the case to the European Court of Human Rights. As a result of this court case, the British Government was forced to pay heavy compensation.

Above: *These are two Tupac Amaru terrorists in the Japanese Embassy in Lima. Terrorist organizations transcend international boundaries and therefore the response has to be multi-national.*

In many instances the SAS is invited to a terrorist incident purely to give advice. Such a case took place on Tuesday 17 December 1996. In this instance 14 Peruvian rebels of the *Tupac Amaru* group, known by the Spanish initials MRTA, stormed the Japanese Embassy in Lima. The surprise attack occurred while the embassy was awash with dignitaries as diplomats, Peruvian government officials and business leaders attended a party celebrating the Japanese emperor's birthday. In all some 600 people, most of whom were VIPs, were enjoying the party when the assault began. According to accounts provided by hostages who were later released, the guerrillas entered between 20:15 and 20:25 hours, just as many of the guests were working their way down the buffet table set up in a tent in the grounds. An explosion followed by a volley of gunfire announced the takeover.

It has never been established exactly how the rebels gained access to the embassy, but reports indicated that most of them simply stormed over the high concrete walls which surround the embassy compound. Other unconfirmed reports said that they entered disguised as waiters, while one newspaper described how the rebels had spent three months tunnelling their way into the grounds of the residence. Whatever their method of entry, the MRTA rebels had certainly researched their target and timed their attack to perfection. The hostage list read like a "Who's Who", and included Peru's foreign minister, Francisco Tudela, the

agriculture minister, Rodolfo Munante Sanguineti, and the speaker of the parliament. Also caught up in the assault were Peru's Supreme Court president, Moises Pantoja, and at least three Peruvian legislators, as well as Japan's ambassador, Morihisa Aoki, and 17 Japanese Embassy staff members. The ambassadors of Austria, Brazil, Bulgaria, Cuba, Guatemala,

Left: *A gun battle in northern Afghanistan. A Northern Alliance fighter engages Taliban forces during the British and American build-up in the country after the terrorist attacks on New York.*

Below: *SAS soldiers arrive in Cyprus en route to Afghanistan in late 2001. The Regiment's expertise in desert warfare has made it ideally suited for operations against Bin Laden's fighters.*

Panama, Poland, Romania, South Korea, Spain and Venezuela, together with seven Americans, were also unlucky enough to have received invitations to the party. Without doubt the hostage list was the best ever taken in any terrorist action, although many guests managed to avoid being captured during the raid. Fernando Andrade, the mayor of the Miraflores section of Lima, escaped by sneaking into a bathroom and then climbing out of a window. US Ambassador Dennis Jett was at the party but left around 19:45 hours, about half an hour before the terrorist attack.

Those who were taken hostage were immediately divided into groups and ushered into rooms on the second floor of the residence.

The ambassadors were separated and held in one room, which was heavily guarded by the rebels. Despite a pitched gun battle during the takeover and the guerrillas' threats, by nightfall the siege had resulted in no deaths and only minor injuries. Once the siege had settled down the rebels issued their demands via a telephone call to a local radio station: 1. Release of some 300 imprisoned rebels, including *Tupac Amaru's* leader, Victor Polay, who had been in solitary confinement for the past four years. 2. Transfer of the freed prisoners and the hostage takers to a jungle hideout with their hostages, the hostages to be released once they had reached their destination. 3. Payment of an unspecified amount as a "war tax". 4. An economic programme to help Peru's poor.

Above: SAS 110 Land Rovers in the 1991 Gulf War. Ten years later the same vehicles would be operating in a similar environment against Al Qaeda terrorists.

Although the demands centred on the release of imprisoned rebels, there was also strong reference to what the rebels called Japan's "constant interference with Peru's internal politics".

In response, the Peruvian Government and the president, Alberto Fujimori, who is of Japanese descent, reminded the world that they had sworn never to negotiate with terrorists. Fujimori, who was elected president in 1990, had managed to severely weaken the guerrilla movements, capturing most of their leaders and jailing thousands of militants and sympathizers. The takeover of the Japanese Embassy now put Peru's

Above: *An SAS Land Rover packed up and ready for deployment anywhere in the world. Note the sand channel attached to the side of the vehicle for traversing soft ground.*

image at stake. It was because of President Fujimori's hard-line action in the past that Japan had invested so heavily in Peru, leading to the *Tupac Amaru*'s resentment of Japanese influence on their country. With so much in the balance, Fujimori spent most of his time presiding over a closed-door meeting of his Council of Ministers, including the chief of police, Kentin Vidal, a legendary figure who had led the successful operation to capture the rebel leader Abimael Guzman.

Twenty-four hours into the siege, when medicine was delivered to the embassy, the rebels released four diplomats: the ambassadors of Canada,

Germany and Greece, and the French cultural attaché. The men read out a statement in which they said they had been sent to "search for a negotiated solution" that would avoid deaths. During the next few days the rebels released more hostages, including President Fujimori's mother and sister. In return, Christmas turkeys were allowed to be delivered to the besieged embassy. Fujimori, however, rejected an opportunity to make a separate deal for other relatives trapped in the embassy and flatly refused to release Peru's guerrilla prisoners. Instead, he offered the terrorists safe passage to some location outside Peru as an incentive for them to lay down their arms and free all their hostages. The rebels refused and set several deadlines, each accompanied by the threat to kill hostages. All these deadlines passed without the loss of life.

By 6 January 1997, the rebels were becoming agitated and refused to release any further hostages until the government started negotiations. Peru's security forces could not dislodge the guerrillas. They did, however, start to implement anti-terrorist procedures. All utility services were disconnected and the government refused to allow fuel into the residence for the generator that had provided power after the electricity had been cut off. The Peruvian authorities ignored repeated demands to restore running water and telephone connections.

As the weeks went by, the Peruvian intelligence services started to monitor activities in the embassy, setting up a series of listening devices. The CIA sent

Above: *SAS soldiers in Afghanistan used the 5.56mm Minimi light machine gun. This lightweight weapon has a practical rate of fire of 85 rounds per minute. The magazine holds 200 rounds.*

a US RG-8A aircraft with a forward-looking infrared camera to monitor the remaining 72 hostages and their 14 rebel guards. The 9.5m (29ft) single-engined aircraft makes very little noise and, in addition to its infrared camera, carries several high-resolution television cameras. The information gathered through these and other observation techniques was vital before any planned assault could take place. It is also believed that one of the hostages, a former military officer, was using a concealed two-way radio to supply information about the rebels. While to this day both the United States and Great Britain deny any direct role in the rescue operation, both supplied experts in anti-terrorism training to Peru, including the SAS. And remember, this was no ordinary terrorist incident. The taking of so many foreign nationals forced many countries to become involved. Some openly offered help.

The British ambassador to Peru, John Illman, voiced Britain's concern: "We are ready to respond and are, in fact, making preparations in advance to

Above: *Northern Alliance members in Afghanistan. The SAS and US special forces worked closely with these fighters during their operations against Taliban and Al Qaeda forces.*

Left: *An Al Qaeda fighter photographed near Kandahar in late 2001. In general, bin Laden's troops were well equipped and motivated, and proved tenacious foes.*

respond to any such request. And we've made it clear that the experience that we have is totally at the disposal of the Peruvian authorities should they require it." This response came in the guise of four members of the British SAS: four specialists whose expertise in the world of counter-terrorism was unparalleled. Their brief was to evaluate the situation and offer solutions. Ultimately, all of their solutions involved an assault of some form. In this case there was a choice of two primary actions: 1. Assault the embassy. 2. Assault the rebels while in transit to freedom.

While the military planned and gathered information, the politicians tried to work out some form of compromise, one of which was to release the rebels and give them asylum in Cuba. To this end President Fujimori had talks with the Cuban president, Fidel Castro. Some 11 weeks into the siege, a basic agreement was in place whereby a military aircraft would take the rebels to Cuba. Whether or not this was a deception or a plan to assault the rebels en route, we shall never know. For while these discussions were taking place, another plan was being conceived by the shadowy figure of the unofficial head of Peruvian intelligence, Ivan Vladimiro Montesinos.

Freeing the Hostages

Montesinos is a cashiered army captain, with a terrifying reputation, and a figure who inspires fear and fascination in Peru. He has not appeared before news cameras for several years but the fact that, wearing dark glasses, he strode victoriously into the liberated Japanese compound with the army chief-of-staff once the siege was over was an obvious indication of his involvement. In reality, it was Montesinos who had raised the 150-man commando unit that carried out the hostage-rescue mission. Using his strong personality, he was able to recruit a combination of the best of the élite special forces

units from the police and army, and get President Fujimori's permission to use them in a daring plan.

Montesinos's plan was to tunnel under the embassy from several different directions, then at the right moment the assaulting force would blast its way through the floor and walls. To facilitate the plan, 24 miners were brought in from the government-owned Centromin mining company. Over a period of several weeks they excavated several tunnels from nearby buildings, each tunnel running to a precise position under the Japanese Embassy. This was not an easy task, as the work needed to be done in secret with both noise and vibration diversions having to be devised and put into operation. The end result was a series of tunnels all equipped with electric light and ventilation. While the tunnels were being dug, the assembled group of élite commandos was undergoing painstaking training in a crude wooden replica of the ambassador's home in the hills outside Lima. There remained, however, one small problem with the method of entry into the embassy. The final flooring, which was solid concrete, had to be breached. If explosives were used, the blast in the confined space of the tunnel would leave none of the assault force in any fit state to jump out and close with the rebels, added to which was the great danger of a cave-in.

SAS Wall-Breaching Devices

The SAS has for many years contemplated such a problem and has researched and developed a wall-breaching cannon. This ingenious device not only creates a hole, it can do so with the assaulting force standing within a few feet. There is no violent shock-wave to tear the assault team limb from limb or cause the cave-in that would bury them alive. Montesinos's plan was to make a sudden breach into the embassy from five different directions. Twenty of the commandos would enter rapidly through the

Above: Among the weapons the SAS took to Afghanistan in 2001 was the Heckler & Koch MP5 submachine gun, primarily for use within confined spaces such as buildings.

Above: This is the MP5 with its single metal strut stock extended and a maglite attached to the end of the barrel for operation in low-light conditions.

floor while the remainder would enter at ground level through the compound walls. With the entire assault force in position the plan was initiated. On 22 April 1997, at 15:00 hours, after four months of captivity, the hostages heard several explosions rapidly followed by blistering gunfire. The rebels had become lethargic and at the moment of assault half of them had been playing football in the main hall, while some were sleeping upstairs. Those rebels outside the building were killed instantly, while those inside met their fate as the commando team carried out a room-by-room clearance. In all the assault took some 15 minutes.

During the assault only one man, Supreme Court Judge Carlo Giusti Acuna, died after being shot and suffering a heart attack. Two police officers involved in the assault also died, one being a member of the security detail assigned to protect the president's son. In all, 25 hostages received minor wounds with two others requiring surgery. All 14 of the rebels were killed. Although at least two dropped their weapons and were seen by several hostages surrendering to the commandos, in the event the government reported that all the rebels had been killed during the assault. TV footage later showed that some of their bodies had been mutilated and even dismembered by the soldiers. The bodies of the rebels were buried in unmarked graves to prevent closer examination.

The SAS in Afghanistan

The use of SAS troops to help the fight in Afghanistan against the *Al Qaeda* network is a good example of recent SAS operations abroad. The SAS had been in Afghanistan for several weeks when it was ordered by US Central Command in Florida to raid an opium storage plant to the southeast of Kandahar. The heavily guarded target location was said to hold some pure opium worth £50 million. In addition to the opium, it was believed that the large amount of guards (estimated at 80 plus) at the site indicated the possibility of finding some useful *Al Qaeda* intelligence documents. Unfortunately, maps of the area were virtually non-existent and the SAS was forced to rely on aerial photographs which had been taken by an unmanned US spy drone. The American command requested that the site be attacked almost immediately, leaving no time for a close target reconnaissance. This would have enabled the SAS assaulting forces to better determine the strengths and weaknesses of the *Al Qaeda* position and refine their strategy accordingly. Timing also meant that the attack would have to take place during daylight hours, abandoning the element of surprise and the use of technically advanced night-vision equipment.

Heavy Firepower

The SAS mustered two full squadrons, almost 120 men, the largest force it has fielded in a single operation for many years. The final assault was to rest on firepower. To this end the SAS used some 30 "Pink Panthers" (110-series Land Rovers specially made for desert warfare), all heavily armed. The "Pinkies" carried both front- and rear-mounted General Purpose Machine Guns (GPMGs), while the roll-bar was mounted with either a MILAN anti-tank rocket system, or an Mk19 automatic grenade launcher. Logistics support came from 2.5-tonne ACMAC lorries acting as "mother" vehicles. Just prior to the assault the American Air Force would carry out two precision air strikes. These would destroy the drug warehouses but leave the headquarters building intact.

The journey to the target started long before dawn. It was a long trek over dreadful, rocky terrain. As the area was hostile the column was forced to stop at regular intervals and send out scouts. For this they used offroad motorcycles just as they had done in the 1991 Gulf War. Dressed in

Above: *The General Purpose Machine Gun (GPMG) has been in SAS service since the late 1950s. GPMGs were mounted on SAS Land Rovers in Afghanistan.*

light order (no backpack), each SAS man carried his personal weapon, either a Colt assault rifle with an underslung M203 grenade launcher or a Minimi machine gun. During such an assault the SAS prefers to forgo any body armour, depending instead on speed of movement. However, in this instance both body armour and Kevlar helmets were used. Belt equipment consisted mainly of grenades, ammunition, food, water and emergency equipment such as a SARBE beacon with which to call for help. By 10:00 hours the force was within 2km (1.2 miles) of the *Al Qaeda* camp, but the going was slow due to soft sand. Midday saw the start of the action, as half the SAS lined up their "Pinkies" and started to lay down covering fire ready for the other half to assault.

The *Al Qaeda* rebels had chosen their defensive positions well. By 13:00 hours a serious firefight had developed, but the assaulting squadron continued to push forward. The attack was helped at this stage by the arrival of US F-16 jets. Their first pass caused massive explosions in and around the compound, but as requested they didn't touch the building serving as the headquarters. The second air strike came close to wiping out the assaulting

force. Despite the horrendous fire put down by the SAS, the *Al Qaeda* fighters refused to give ground, preferring to die. But by 14:30 hours most resistance had been overwhelmed and the headquarters raided for laptop computers, papers and maps. The ground was littered with dead *Al Qaeda* fighters, with those that were wounded screaming for Allah.

On the SAS side several men had been hit, but thanks to the body armour and Kevlar helmets most of the wounds were to the limbs. That said, several injuries were extremely serious and required all the skills of the SAS medics to keep the injured alive. Finally, the word was sent to "bug-out". Everyone jumped back in their vehicles and headed south. The first port of call was a rendezvous at a makeshift airfield, where a C-130 complete with doctors and medics evacuated the wounded, flying them directly back to the UK. Although several of the wounded were in a serious condition, the mission had been accomplished without the loss of a single SAS soldier.

CHAPTER 6

Victories at Home

For the SAS Anti-Terrorist Team, Northern Ireland proved to be a difficult and dangerous place in which to work. Over the years the Regiment has achieved some spectacular results in its fight against the terrorists of the Irish Republican Army.

Despite the fact that the Anti-Terrorist Team was formed to protect the interests of Great Britain, many of the early SAS operations involved helping other nations within Western Europe. While SAS soldiers rotated through the Anti-Terrorist Team on an annual basis, they also did their tour of duty in Northern Ireland. Those soldiers serving their time in Ulster put the training received while on the team into actual practice during operations. This made Northern Ireland a perfect proving ground for counter-terrorist tactics and equipment.

There is no doubt that the SAS has learned much from its years in Northern Ireland, and it was interesting to see how operational procedure developed. The initial and notorious SAS cross-border operations were all carried out in camouflage uniform, with tactics very similar to an infantry role. But 20 years in the Province produced a sharp contrast. Most recent SAS operations were conducted undercover, carrying out surveillance or Close Target Reconnaissance (CTR) of one type or

Left: A British Army helicopter approaches a base in South Armagh, Northern Ireland. This area was the scene of intense SAS activity during the 1970s and 1980s.

another. Even though this was a dramatic change it was also part of the Regiment's evolution, not just in Northern Ireland but also in mainland UK. However, as we have seen recently in Afghanistan, the SAS soldier fighting in the "Special Forces" role is still with us, but more and more the Regiment is being used for covert operations. Its expertise is spreading into espionage, counter-drugs and even civilian law enforcement.

Fighting the IRA

The first encounter between the Irish Republican Army (IRA) and the Anti-Terrorist Team happened on 6 December 1975. After attacking a restaurant, a four-man active service unit of the IRA took a middle-aged couple hostage in a flat in Balcombe Street, London. Armed police were on the scene almost immediately, and Scotland Yard was able to monitor the proceedings in the flat using fibre-optic cameras inserted into the walls. However, the gunmen held their ground and the siege, which reached its eighth day, looked as if it was going to continue indefinitely. Inside the flat, the terrorists were able to listen to a transistor radio and heard a report from the BBC suggesting that an SAS unit was preparing to intervene and take over the building. Scaffold screening was being erected outside to ward off the prying eyes of the media. Upon seeing this activity and hearing the news on the radio, the terrorists immediately surrendered to the police. Unofficially the SAS has had men in Northern Ireland since 1973, but most of these were just short visits, often where an SAS man would be attached to a local infantry regiment. Then, in 1976,

Above: The early days in Northern Ireland were spent patrolling the border area in South Armagh. This photograph shows where a command wire to an IRA bomb had been laid.

it became a political tool, sent to the Province to curb the sudden increase in IRA violence.

Tit-for-tat killings took place almost on a daily basis, much of the bloodshed being directed against innocent civilians of the opposing religious factions. In the end the British Government ordered the SAS to take action. The climate changed when, on 12 March, a known IRA member, Sean McKenna, was lifted from his home over the border by an SAS team. He was dragged from his bed, quickly dressed and frog-marched into the North, whereupon he was handed over to the Royal Ulster Constabulary (RUC). Less than a month later another IRA member, Peter Cleary, was lifted from the home of his fiancée, who lived just north of the

border. The house had been under observation for some time, and knowing that Cleary was soon to be married, it was just a matter of waiting. Once Cleary had been taken into captivity, the SAS patrol moved to a pick-up point and waited for its helicopter. During this time Cleary tried to escape, and he was shot dead. The incident did not go down well. The IRA claimed that he had been murdered. Several senior officers in Northern Ireland were aghast at having the SAS in their midst, but as the government had sent the Regiment there was little they could do.

Despite personal opinion the situation did serve to send a message to the IRA: over the border or not, we will come and get you. This theory was confirmed when, at around 18:00 hours on the evening of 5 May 1976, the Gardai stopped two men in a car at a checkpoint within the Irish Republic. To make matters worse, two back-up vehicles

Above: *The MP5K is a shortened version of the MP5 submachine gun. At 325mm (12.7in) in length it was used by SAS undercover teams in Northern Ireland.*

arrived to assist. In total eight members of the SAS, together with their vehicles and weaponry, were taken into custody by the Gardai. As the news emerged all hell broke loose, and the newspapers had a field day. The men were taken to Dundalk and then on to Dublin; all were charged. In the end it was just as embarrassing to the Irish Republic as it was for the SAS men, most of whom where fined £100 for having unlicensed weapons.

During the late 1970s there were other successes and, as with most violent conflicts, the odd failure. Slowly the Regiment evolved its own strategy, forming stronger links with the RUC Special Branch. This link provided crisper information for the SAS to work upon. One significant operation came in June 1978, when information was received that an IRA cell was about to bomb the Post Office depot in Belfast.

It was a classic operation. Special Branch had given us the information and we would provide the solution. It was fairly simple: a team of IRA were to fire-bomb the Post Office depot in Belfast. We even knew from which side they would approach and made our plans accordingly. The only thing we did not know was the exact time of the bombing. In the event, several observation posts were set up, the main one being located in a house, which gave a clear view of the small alley that ran to the side of the Post Office compound where the vehicles and utilities were housed. This compound was protected by a high fence. As well as several cut-off groups secreted around the compound, a reaction team, sitting in a van, lay in wait. I hate to think how many hours I spent lying in that van; it was bloody uncomfortable. As the operation progressed into several days, it was deemed a better idea to establish two guys in a large bush during the hours of darkness. On the night in question the task fell to Tony and Jim (not their real names). Tony was in my troop, and a better man is hard to find. He was solidly built, laid back and very cool. In this incident and many others in years to come, when the chips were down he was the man to have by your side.

The Terrorists Attack

The other guy, Jim, was a little younger and not quite so level-headed. The SAS guy in the observation house was bored. He had sat at the window for several days, and nothing had happened. Special Branch had reassured him several times that the bombing would take place, but as time went on he was having doubts. Then, suddenly, he saw the figures in the alley. They were almost touching the wall of the compound. Before he could raise the alarm one of the figures moved his arm – the first bomb was already arching its way towards the target. "GO! GO! GO!" The operation was on.

With Tony in the lead, the two men leapt from the bush. The light on top of Tony's MP5 submachine gun sent out a beam; in front of him were three figures, two of them about to throw satchel bombs. Tony fired two short bursts – two men fell dead. The third made a run for it, retreating back down the alley, from the direction he had come. Tony fired another short burst and the man fell. Perfect, but for the fact that Jim, who on this occasion was armed with an automatic SLR, decided to confirm the kills – a lot of heavy-calibre rounds were fired. Almost as Jim finished firing, two men entered the alley from the bottom end. Immediately, Tony called out a challenge, unsure as to the identity of the men. One dropped to the ground and placed his hands on his head, the other made a run for it. He never made it. A short burst from Tony killed him.

As the situation cleared, it turned out that the two men were just returning from the pub and had accidentally walked straight into the firefight. Had the man, a Protestant by the name of William Hanna, remained still after the challenge, he would be alive today. And I can assure you a clear challenge was given. Without going into too much detail, I will say that the problems really started when the lawyers and legal officers arrived. The weapons were tagged and taken away for forensic examination. Then each man gave his story. It was all clear and simple until the lawyer asked Jim to give his account in his own words. "Well, I saw Tony move and I backed him up. He slotted two, but the third made a run for it. As Tony fired, I stepped to one side and shouted to the boys in the bottom cut-off. 'Keep your head down Bobby,' then I let rip with a 30-round mag." The legal officer looked in horror at such a statement, while the rest of us just rolled around laughing. His story was corrected, and no court case followed.

Not long after, Special Branch in Armagh tasked the SAS unit in Portadown to recce a Catholic church in Castleford (name changed). The essence of the information was that there were IRA meetings taking place in a small building at the rear of the church grounds. Special Branch wanted the SAS to have a look and photograph any documents of interest. Two men were trusted with the task, one of them a lock-picking specialist. They were driven to the town by two other SAS personnel, who would stay mobile in the area and act as back-up. At around 01:00 hours on a wet and windy morning, the two men were dropped off by a gateway at the edge of the town, and quickly made their way to the rear of the church.

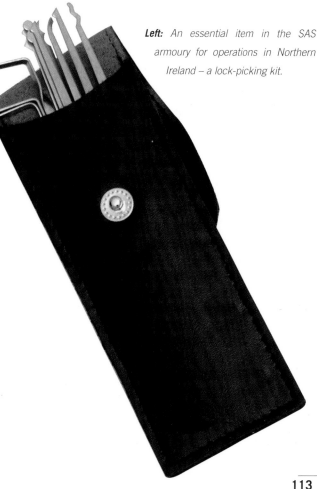

Left: An essential item in the SAS armoury for operations in Northern Ireland – a lock-picking kit.

The whole church was surrounded on three sides by a 3.9m (12ft) wall, with iron railings to the road-side front. Approaching from the rear, the two men quickly climbed the wall and in the shadow of the church approached the meeting house.

A Rich Haul

The small, two-storey building stood in one rear corner, with one window and a single door to the bottom floor. One of the SAS men produced a set of picks and made short work of the padlock. Inside the ground floor was searched; there was nothing of interest as much of the space was taken up with church paraphernalia. A small set of stairs led to the second floor; this was also barred by a padlock. This upper floor had two windows, allowing the room to be illuminated by the street lighting. It contained several lockers filled with paperwork and books; in the centre was a large table and several chairs. They carried out a search of the room and the cupboards but little of interest was found, certainly no reference to the IRA. A small trap door leading to the loft was discovered, and by placing a chair on the table, this could be reached. Checking the hatchway for any booby traps, one of the SAS men climbed inside. After he had secured the hatch behind him, he put on his torch. What confronted him was a whole mess of large plastic bags, most of which contained bomb-making equipment. Several pounds of Semtex plastic explosive was discovered, as were 20 ready-to-go cassette incendiaries. The information was relayed directly back to control and an observation unit was organized for the next day.

Unfortunately, when Special Branch found out the situation changed. For some unexplained reason, MI5 became involved. This meant no SAS anywhere near the building, and the target was electronically tagged. The two SAS men had the pleasure of taking the MI5 operative into the building. The problem was he was so fat that he demolished half the rear wall climbing over it. Additionally, he could not pick the lock and required an expert (the SAS man had the lock open in seconds). For the SAS that was the end of the story, well for three weeks anyway. Then a call came from Special Branch to remove all the explosives and bury them in a hide. The hide was to look like an IRA job and be at least half a mile from the church. This was done, and next day an SAS soldier stood on the site as the local Ulster Defence Regiment (UDR) searched the area. "It's

Right: A rather wet and miserable SAS soldier after an observation mission in Northern Ireland. Much reconnaissance work involves lying in ditches and holes for days at a time.

here mate," said the SAS man. Next day in the papers, the headlines read of a major explosives find by the UDR. There was a reason. It told the IRA, who had put the explosives in the church, that it was being watched. In the eyes of the general public, it also made the British Army look good.

A Testing Time in Ulster

There was also a time in Northern Ireland when nothing seemed to go right for the SAS. April 1980 was a perfect example. The SAS in South Armagh had been tasked with several jobs all at the same time. The first was to set up an observation post (OP) watching the home of two men of the RUC, whose lives had been threatened. The second was to keep watch on a public house the IRA intended to fire-bomb. Finally, a well-known IRA terrorist intended to shoot a man at a dance. The man was suspected of being an informer, and the SAS task was to keep tabs on both gunman and target. These three operations called for reinforcements and so more SAS men were drafted into South Armagh. Four men went into the first OP watching the two RUC policemen. Four more

Below: In Ireland SAS soldiers dressed in standard British Army uniforms without any regimental insignia. Thus they were able to blend into routine army operations.

went into the OP at the pub but, due to a shortage of numbers, this OP was pulled off during the operation against the would-be IRA assassin and his target.

This operation required at least six cars, each containing two men and several men in the dance hall or pub. In addition to all this, we needed men for drop-offs, resupply, Quick Reaction Forces (QRFs) and to man the operations room. Things started going wrong when after a week the OP watching the RUC policemen was compromised by a farmer, and asked to be extracted. Special Branch was informed of this, and pleaded with the SAS team to stay put. The commander of the OP made a decision, and as in all SAS operations the man in the field calls the shots – they were withdrawn. Next morning, as the two RUC policemen returned home from work, their car was shot-up, spent cartridge cases were found just a few metres from where the SAS OP had been. Luckily the two RUC policemen were untouched. A week later, as the OP on the public house was withdrawn to help with the surveillance on the would-be assassin, the second disaster happened.

By 02:00 hours on a Sunday morning, both the IRA gunman and his target had been followed and finally housed without any incident taking place. As the cars drove back to Portadown Barracks, their

Above: An early photograph of IRA terrorists, 1970. Don't be fooled by the comic appearance, the IRA is a well-armed, well-trained terrorist organization with access to modern hardware.

route home took them past the pub that had been under observation. It was burning. By this time Special Branch was not very pleased with the SAS. Operations, however, continued. In Belfast, it was discovered that weapons under observation had been moved. Unfortunately, their new home was a bit of a mystery; the nearest location that could be found was a block of three houses in a terraced row on the Antrim Road. After a check with intelligence,

it turned out that one of the three houses had been previously used by the IRA, so this house was therefore targeted.

On the afternoon of 2 May, two cars headed down the Antrim Road and screeched to a stop outside No 369. Another vehicle containing three SAS men secured the rear. For security reasons there had been no cordon or military activity prior to the raid, and the SAS men went straight in. The lead groups were already in the house and up the stairs when a burst of automatic gunfire filled the air. Unknown to the SAS team, the IRA had mounted an American M60 machine gun in the upstairs window of the adjoining house. The boys had moved in fast but the commander, Captain Westmacott, who had been sitting in the middle of the rear seat, was the last to move. He was shot dead by a burst from the M60. Realizing what was happening the whole assault was quickly switched, but by this time the IRA man had surrendered. The sound of gunfire brought the army and RUC to the scene, additionally a Catholic priest suddenly materialized to see that the IRA man was allowed to surrender. Other suspects leaving by the back door were arrested and several weapons were also recovered.

Throughout this spate of disasters there was one shining light – the assault by the SAS on the Iranian Embassy in London (see Chapter 3). For the first time the public saw the black-clad men of the Anti-Terrorist Team in action. The successful action in London also negated some of the misgivings that Northern Ireland Special Branch was beginning to have about the SAS.

Major Successes

Not all SAS operations were directed against the IRA. When it was discovered that the Protestant Ulster Defence Association (UDA), for example, intended to kill the Republican activist and former MP, Bernadette McAliskey (née Devlin), the SAS mounted an operation to prevent it. Intelligence indicated that the UDA planned to kill McAliskey, together with her husband Michael, at their isolated farmhouse near Coalisland on 6 January 1981. SAS men put the house under observation but the nearest they could conceal themselves was some 200m (609ft) from the building. When the three gunmen arrived by car, they did so at speed, driving directly up to the house. The SAS team responded immediately, but by the time they reached the house the UDA had smashed the door in and shots were heard. The gunmen were arrested

as they made their escape, and on checking inside the house the soldiers found Michael McAliskey bleeding from a severed artery and in a grave condition. Bernadette, although shot several times, was not so critical. The SAS medic kept them both alive until an ambulance arrived. The McAliskeys survived and the three UDA assassins were given long prison sentences.

On Friday 8 May 1987, the SAS hit the jackpot. Intelligence had been received to indicate that the police station at Loughall was to be attacked by a method used a year before in County Armagh. That incident had taken place in April 1986, when a mechanical digger had been packed with explosives and driven into the RUC station at the Birches and the explosives detonated. The attack had caused widespread damage. A report that another JCB had been stolen in East Tyrone created suspicions that an identical IRA operation was being planned. All efforts were made to locate the digger and identify the target. After intensive covert searching, the weapons and explosives were located. Subsequently, the digger was also located in a derelict building on a farm some 15km (9.3 miles) away.

Ambush at Loughall

Surveillance by E4A provided more information, and eventually the target was confirmed as the RUC station at Loughall. The RUC station was only manned part-time, and consisted of one main building running parallel to the main road and surrounded by a high wire fence. The time and date of the attack was eventually confirmed through a Special Branch telephone tap. Two of the IRA activists were named as Patrick Kelly and Jim Lynagh, who commanded the East Tyrone active service unit. When masked men stole a Toyota van from Dungannon, Jim Lynagh was spotted in the town, leading to the possibility that the van was to be used in the Loughall attack. Not long after, the OP reported that the JCB was being moved from the derelict farm.

At this stage the SAS, who had been reinforced from Hereford, took up their ambush positions. It was reported that some were in the police station itself, but this was not true. Instead, most of the main ambush party was hiding in a row of small fir trees that lines the fence on the opposite side to the station. Several heavily armed stops were also in position covering all avenues of escape. At a little past 19:00 hours, the blue Toyota van drove down the road in front of the police station. Several people were seen to be inside. It shortly returned from the direction of Portadown, this time followed by the JCB with three hooded IRA terrorists in the cab. Declan Arthurs was driving, with Michael Gormley and Gerald O'Callaghan as passengers. The bucket was filled with explosives contained in an oil drum; this had been partly concealed with rubble. While the blue van charged past the station, the JCB slammed through the gate.

A Bloody Firefight

One of the two passengers, it was not clear which one, set the bomb for detonation and all three made a run for it. Back at the van, several hooded men jumped clear and started to open fire in the direction of the RUC station. The SAS ambush was activated. The sudden torrent of SAS fire was terrifying. All eight members of the IRA fell under a hail of bullets. At the height of the firefight the bomb exploded, taking with it half the RUC station and scattering debris over all concerned. As the dust settled, the SAS closed in on the bodies. At that moment a white car entered the ambush area. Both the occupants, dressed in blue boiler suits similar to those worn by the IRA, were unfortunately mistaken for terrorists. It did not help their cause that on seeing the ambush in

progress, they stopped and started to reverse. One of the SAS stop teams opened fire, killing one of the occupants and wounding the other. It later transpired that the dead motorist, Antony Hughes, had nothing to do with the IRA.

Several other vehicles and pedestrians soon appeared on the scene, but by this time the situation was stabilized. For this quiet village, it was an incredible sight: the RUC station half demolished; the mangled yellow metal that was once a JCB, and the numerous bodies littering the street. Without doubt, Loughall was one of the most successful operations ever mounted against the IRA, who were totally stunned by the loss of two complete active service cells. The Hughes family were compensated for their loss, and with no public inquest, the matter was closed. The IRA, believing there was a mole in its organization, went into a period of self-assessment, but did not lick its wounds for long. Shortly after, on Remembrance Day at a ceremony in Enniskillen, the IRA detonated a massive bomb. Eleven were killed, and more than 60 were injured.

Peterhead Prison

The SAS has been given some curious jobs in its time. For example, on 27 September 1987 a siege erupted in D Block of Peterhead Prison in Scotland. The block held some 48 prisoners, most of whom where serving long-term sentences for murder and rape. The majority of the prisoners gave themselves up after a short while, but a hard core of five men holding a prison officer hostage totally refused to surrender. For the following week the rioters paraded on the rooftop in full view of the world's media. The Grampian Police responded with a specialist response team, and the government ordered two SAS advisors to assist. A quick assessment of the situation promoted the idea that the task should be better dealt with by an SAS

Above: The death of Captain Westmacott was mainly due to the lack of assault speed and poor intelligence. He was shot dead just as the SAS assault was about to raid an IRA safe house.

Right: The Irish Republican activist Bernadette McAliskey was targeted for assassination by the Protestant Ulster Defence Association. She was saved by the SAS.

team, who were better versed in such assault tactics. The government finally gave its consent for the SAS assault on the morning of 3 October.

At around 04:00 hours, a four-man team armed with batons instead of submachine guns made its way from a skylight across a slippery roof to the hole that had previously been made by the rioters. They dropped both stun grenades and CS gas through the hole before dropping in themselves to confront the prisoners. At the same time, back-up teams made an explosive entry through the lower floor walls and proceeded to follow up the roof assault. The hostage was the first to be removed, too weak to help himself. The assault team on the

roof hauled him through the hole and carried him back to the skylight, where he was lowered to safety. The prisoners, overwhelmed by CS gas and the black-clad figures, obeyed the bellowing commands to "move" as they were marshalled back into captivity. The SAS assault team departed from Scotland less than two hours after its arrival, having successfully completed the mission. As a result of the Peterhead Prison riot, the government set up a specialist team to deal with such incidents. These officers were initially trained in Hereford.

Boeing 727 Hijacked by Afghans

Although this operation turned out to be a bit of a farce, the SAS Anti-Terrorist Team treated it as it would any other hijack in Britain. The Ariana Boeing 727 had been hijacked shortly after it took off from Kabul on a domestic run to Mazar-e-Sharif. It arrived at London's Stanstead Airport early on Monday morning after a dramatic journey via Uzbekistan, Kazakhstan and Russia. What most people would have missed was the position in which the aircraft was parked. As I mentioned in Chapter 3, the SAS has contingency plans for just such an incident. That's why the aircraft was routed to Stanstead instead of Heathrow – the aircraft was placed in the exact spot as part of a pre-defined plan.

Sniper and assault positions are all pre-determined, and in this case the hijackers went along with what was requested of them. As the days went by there seemed to be no serious political demands, and it appeared that the hijackers were uncertain how to proceed. Several days into the negotiations and the flight crew had escaped. By that time I knew that it would end peacefully and believed the hijackers to be asylum

Left: *The aftermath of the SAS ambush at Loughall, May 1987. The terrorists' blue Toyota van can be seen in the bottom left-hand corner of the photograph.*

seekers. (I told this to a BBC correspondent but he was not interested.) From the limited information available, it seemed to me that the hijackers were keen to save their own skins. However, by this time I had decided to return home to Spain, confident that the police negotiator would soon announce the hijackers' surrender.

The day-to-day control of any hijack is firmly under the guidance of the regional chief constable, in this case David Stephens of the Essex police force. He deployed 150 officers, many of them armed, around the aircraft at any one time. Scotland Yard lent 30 to 40 specialist firearms officers, including long-range snipers from SO19. This police section is equipped and armed in a similar manner to the SAS, and deals with matters deemed not to require the SAS's specialist talents. The London force also sent dogs, officers and armour-plated Land Rovers from its tactical support group. The SAS only becomes involved when the police ask for its assistance.

The End of the Hijack

The hijackers of the 727 started to set free yet more hostages, having already released a total of 22 hostages in return for supplies during earlier stops in Uzbekistan, Kazakhstan and Russia. On 10 February 2000 it was all over, with the release of the remaining 150 passengers and crew. The first group of 85 were released just after 03:00 hours, these including women and 20 or so children. Just after 06:00 hours another group of 65 people, mostly men, walked off the plane. This group included the hijackers. In all some 19 people were arrested on suspicion of involvement in the hijack. The police searched the aircraft and found four handguns, five knives, two detonators and two grenades without fuses. At least 60 of the passengers have applied for asylum and, under international law, Great Britain is obliged to consider an application for political asylum, even from hijackers.

CHAPTER 7

Training Others

The SAS is in great demand for its counter-terrorist expertise, both from British agencies and foreign states. As a result, SAS soldiers can be found all over the world training the anti-terrorist teams of friendly nations in the skills of hostage-rescue and anti-terrorism.

The SAS Anti-Terrorist Team is permanently garrisoned at Credenhill, Herefordshire. Being based in Hereford for a few months is always welcome, as it means a stable family life for the married men and a chance to arrange a social life for those who are single. While the evenings and weekends may be blissful, the working day for an anti-terrorist operator can be quite hectic. The team must be maintained at a very high standard, with new members being introduced to the workings of a modern anti-terrorist organization. All members will need to reaffirm their basic skills with individual shooting practice. Tactics for every terrorist scenario are normally honed during several exercises.

There is also an endless procession of VIPs that visit the SAS in Credenhill, and they frequently become the live hostages in the "snatch" scenario. Out of respect for security, I will refrain from naming any specific persons, but the list of VIP names is very long. It ranges from foreign heads of

Left: SAS bodyguard training in action. The training facilities of the Regiment are excellent. They range from full-sized aircraft to deep underground bunkers housing a variety of ranges.

Above: An amused Princess Anne being bundled out of the "Killing House" by members of the Anti-Terrorist Team. Many members of the Royal Family undergo similar training.

state to more familiar home-grown dignitaries who have requested to see the SAS in action. The same demonstration, which is practised as part of the anti-terrorist hostage-rescue scenario, is used for just about every visit. This demonstration serves a number of purposes, the most important one being to train all visiting VIPs in what they can expect if they are ever the beneficiary of a hostage-rescue operation. To this end the SAS Anti-Terrorist Team usually insists that the VIP plays the role of a hostage during the snatch scenario. The hostage finds himself or herself sitting in absolute darkness, surrounded by silence, not knowing what

possessed him to volunteer in the first place. This stage is bad enough. Abruptly, the door bursts open and a stun grenade explodes in the room. Black-clad figures burst into the darkened room firing live rounds at targets positioned within inches of him. Now petrified, the hostage sits in terrified stillness as beams from gun-mounted lasers penetrate the blackness, searching hungrily for targets. He must not move. Any movement might bring him into contact with the hail of bullets around him. It's unqualified fear. Luckily, he is plucked, albeit roughly, by the black-clad figures and literally thrown out of the room, surprised later to discover not a single scratch upon his person.

VIPs normally come with an entourage of hangers-on. During the demonstration they are normally in the same room as the hostage snatch, securely trapped in the corner behind a strip of white tape (a no-fire area). There is an excellent cartoon hanging up in the "Killing House", which shows the boys bursting into the room and shooting the wrong way, while the instructor's voice booms over the loudspeaker: "No! No! – shoot the targets."

SAS Training Facilities

Team members with several years' experience may be selected for training specialist police squads or military units. As the SAS possesses some of the best training facilities in the world, it is only logical that such training takes place at one of their special camps in and around Hereford. Such courses can range from VIP protection, high-speed driving, demolition or basic anti-terrorist techniques.

The training facilities available to the SAS are state-of-the-art. Where secrecy is demanded training will normally take place at a hidden location. These are known only by number, "Camp One" for example, and the actual name of the location is never mentioned. At these locations it is possible to train away from the prying eyes of the

Above: *The SAS Anti-Terrorist Team pose with Princess Diana and Prince Charles during one of their visits to Hereford. Royal bodyguards are now trained by the SAS.*

media, or anyone else who feels a strong desire to see the SAS in action. Many of the facilities are in underground bunkers not dissimilar to large underground car parks. Where the facilities are above ground, large trees have been grown which obscure vision up to a height of 5m (15ft). Security is tight, and everyone is monitored by hidden cameras. If you linger for more than a few minutes or produce a camera, armed policemen will suddenly descend on you and at the very least you will spend the night in prison. Camp One also has a purpose-built embassy which is used to practise building assaults at various levels. Several full-

sized aircraft can also be found in the grounds, together with a platform which passes for an oil rig. Bus and train assault options are practised, as are high-speed car drills. There is even a range where live-firing anti-ambush drills are taught.

Although designed primarily for the SAS, other friendly nations, especially the United States, are often found taking advantage of these facilities. Since the relocation to Credenhill the SAS has added several major features to its training arsenal, but these must remain secret. The new camp also offers the facility to bring in large aircraft, such as C-130 heavy transports.

A perfect example of why the SAS trains other British forces derives from an incident that happened in the early 1970s. At the time many Royal VIPs felt they could travel around Great

Britain with little or no security. Many had bodyguards, true, but at the time these were chosen more for their suitability to handle social demands than to react against a terrorist incident. At times many members of the Royal Family would drive from Buckingham Palace to Windsor without any escort or back-up. With terrorism on the increase in Western Europe, this was an accident waiting to happen – and it did.

Terror on the Mall

On the night of 20 March 1974, Princess Anne and her husband, Captain Mark Phillips, were driving down the Mall in London, accompanied by Inspector Jim Beaton. Beaton was of the old school: neat appearance and well educated. On this occasion, he was armed – unfortunately his gun did not work. He had joined the Royal Protection Group a year earlier, where he had been trained on the 9mm Walther PPK pistol. At the time the Royal Protection Group, which consisted of about 20 men, fired little more than a few hundred rounds during training; refresher training consisted of about 50 rounds. Compared to an SAS bodyguard, this training was minimal. As any good shot will tell you, the more you shoot, the more proficient you become.

Despite its limitations in magazine capacity (it holds seven rounds), the Walther PPK is a slim-fitting weapon, and has been used by the SAS. I personally carried one for years in Northern Ireland. It is well suited to operating in civilian clothes and is better concealed than the bulky Browning Hi-Power. Used with precision, it was one of the finest weapons around at the time. Its main fault, if it had one, was the magazine. If this was not emptied on a regular basis, thus allowing the spring to relax, stoppages would occur.

On the night in question, the royal party were returning from a charity reception in the city. By 19:50 hours their somewhat old Rolls Royce

limousine was driving up the Mall, just minutes away from Buckingham Palace. At this stage, a white Ford Escort deliberately cut in front of the Rolls, forcing it to stop. There are several different stories about what happened next. The bodyguard, Beaton, thinking it was nothing more than a London lunatic, left his front passenger seat, and walked around the rear of the car, taking up position by the off-side rear door. This put him between the driver of the white Ford, who had now disembarked, and Princess Anne. No sooner had he stopped to survey the situation when a shot rang out from the Ford driver, the bullet hitting Beaton in the chest. Staggering backwards, Beaton immediately sought shelter behind the car. Instinctively, he drew his pistol and fired. There is some argument as to how he did this, but whatever

the case he missed the aggressor. The Princess is later reported to have said the following: "The policeman got off one shot, which I am convinced came through the back window of the car as something hit me on the back of the head. So I thought, that was a good start."

Beaton, although seriously wounded and quickly loosing blood, made another attempt to shoot, but the gun just went "click". In normal circumstances, the correct stoppage drill would have cleared this in seconds. Mechanically he was going through the right motions, but Beaton was clearly not switched on, and as he was wounded his ability to operate was greatly reduced. The chauffeur, Alexander Callender, had seen the driver of the Ford, later revealed as one Ian Ball, deliberately smash into the Rolls. He had also seen Ball step out of the car and produce a gun. After he had shot Beaton, Ball then tried to open the driver's side rear door where the Princess sat.

Both the Princess and Captain Phillips held onto the handle and a tug-of-war ensued. Ball finally managed to get hold of Princess Anne's arm and tried to pull her from the vehicle; she resisted by hanging on to her husband. When the sleeve of her dress came away in Ball's hand, they managed to get the door closed once more. Beaton made another attempt at confronting Ball, but seeing his advantage Ball demanded that the officer put down his weapon. Beaton did so then climbed into the car to sit by the Princess – an act of defiance if nothing else. The lady-in-waiting, Rowena Brassey, who had accompanied the Royal couple, left the vehicle and made to pick up the officer's weapon. It was a gesture of courage, and an honourable one, but cries from the crowd, who were now gathering, persuaded her not to. At that moment, a journalist, John McConnell, having heard the shots fired, arrived on the scene and challenged Ball. Ball's response was to produce a second weapon, a .22 pistol, and shoot McConnell in the chest. The journalist staggered away, and Ball concentrated once more on kidnapping the Princess. He repeatedly threatened Beaton, pointing the pistol at the window, directly at his head. Instinctively knowing that Ball was about to shoot, Beaton put his palm to the window; Ball shot him in the hand. Had Beaton not acted in this way the bullet would have certainly hit the Princess.

A policeman, PC Michael Hills, who had been on duty at nearby St James Palace, had also responded to the shootings. He radioed Cannon Row police station, and at last the authorities were alerted.

Left: The rather unobtrusive brick exterior of the famous "Killing House" at SAS headquarters. Note the paper targets that are used during live-firing drills.

There had been no radio communications fitted to the Rolls Royce, and personal radios were thought to be intrusive by the Royal Protection Group at that time. Arriving at the scene, Hills confronted Ball, only to be shot in the stomach. As he crawled away the chauffeur opened his door and Ball also shot Callender in the chest. By now the situation was becoming critical, and Ball tried once more to open the rear door. As he succeeded, Beaton lashed out with his foot. Ball shot him for a third time.

On seeing this, several "have-a-go merchants" descended on the gunman. One parked his car in front of Ball's, effectively blocking his escape route. Another man, Ronald Russell, who had been passing in a taxi, tackled Ball and managed to punch him. Ball fired but missed. Russell was still fighting with Ball when the police arrived. Ball made a run for it, but was soon tackled by a policeman and captured. Ball was locked away for the duration, and a full inquiry was held into the incident.

Upgrading Royal Defences

One cannot pin blame on men who have been wounded in the line of duty, and just rewards were given out to those involved. The 9mm Walther seemed to be the culprit and was subsequently replaced by the Smith & Western .38 Special. Security improvements were made, such as the installation of radios and bullet-proof glass, and automatic locks in royal vehicles were also fitted. The most outstanding change came when the Head of the Royal Protection Group, Commander Trestrail, visited Hereford in early 1975. He was not given the normal VIP demonstration; instead, he was party to a VIP three-day exercise. It soon became blatantly clear to Trestrail what standards

Left: SAS training camps have airstrips that are large enough to accommodate C-130 Hercules transport aircraft, as seen here. Security is extremely tight around all SAS facilities.

of training existed and what levels of protection could be achieved. After this the Royal Protection Group all came to Hereford for training.

It is not just the British Royal Family that have taken advantage of the SAS. The specialist security units of many friendly nations have, over the years, been trained at Hereford. The SAS role has not been to supply permanent bodyguards, but to train the local forces to do the job. Additionally, since 1975, many ex-SAS soldiers have become bodyguards for the rich and famous, and although the demand has declined it is still the largest single industry for ex-Regiment personnel. The OPEC conference hijack in 1975 did much to initiate this industry. Eleven oil ministers and 59 other hostages were kidnapped in Vienna, flown to Algiers, and only released after the payment of a large ransom. Soon after, several of those oil ministers kidnapped took on SAS bodyguards. At one stage it became so fashionable to have a British SAS bodyguard that the drain on the Regiment was excessive. For some, but not all, there were rich pickings to be had.

The Drain on SAS Manpower

The Thatcher years saw a huge increase in security, and one of the prime minister's first changes was to order several armoured Daimlers. She also increased the number of policemen for the protection of top politicians. The SAS was directly tasked with providing training for this increased manpower, and for a while Hereford became the bodyguard Mecca. In special circumstances, where the risk was thought to be abnormally high, the SAS took over the protection itself. Soviet defectors and "A" listed Ministry of Defence personnel being among the VIPs. The resulting proficiency and know-how has made the SAS a world leader in the fight against terrorism. Because of this its expertise is in demand, and requests for training teams are constantly received by the British Government.

Above: Charles Beckwith was the founder of the US Delta Force anti-terrorist unit. He spent two years in Hereford working with the SAS, during which time he took part in live operations.

However most of these requests, unless deemed a political necessity, are refused. This is not because the SAS does not want to share its hard-earned secrets; it is mainly due to lack of manpower. The SAS is only a small unit and the government or the military constantly uses its soldiers for active duty. What little time they do have in the UK is either taken up with retraining on new equipment or participating in the Anti-Terrorist Team. As I stated earlier, if you are married time at home with your family is always at a premium (the SAS has a very high divorce rate mainly due to the absence of home life). Therefore, the number of overseas training teams has been cut right back. However, there are exceptions.

There has always been a good working relationship between US Special Forces and the SAS, and exchange programmes have been going on since the early 1960s. However, the special link

with Delta Force is down to one man, Colonel Charles Beckwith. Beckwith was a US Special Forces officer who trained with the SAS and saw action in Malaya in the 1950s. He later developed a reputation for ruthlessness and bravery in the Vietnam War, where he commanded a unit known as Project Delta. Later, in 1977, he was given the task of setting up the US's first counter-terrorist unit, which became known as Delta Force. Beckwith based his new unit on the SAS, and indeed the first Delta recruits trained at Hereford. During the Falklands War in 1982 the SAS sent a representative over to Delta for training on the Stinger anti-aircraft missile system, and also arranged for a number of Stingers to find their way down to the Falklands.

The recent conflict in Afghanistan has once again seen both Delta and the SAS working side by side, fostering their relationship even further. It is a link that is vital to the advancement of anti-terrorist techniques and the development of specialist equipment. Additionally, shared information about international terrorist organizations is of benefit to both countries.

The British interest in Saudi Arabia is mainly political, as it ships large quantities of oil to the West. In general, Great Britain maintains good

Above: Members of the Saudi anti-terrorist team practise a bus assault. Less than a year after it was formed, the unit was involved in a successful action in Mecca.

relations with Saudi Arabia and sees the country as a stable influence in the Middle East. It is therefore incumbent on the British to assist in retaining the status quo. Helping to train the country's anti-terrorist team is an excellent way of doing this. It also highlights what an SAS training team does. As I personally took part in the training, I shall explain from my own experience how the training works.

We arrived in Jeddah and were shown to a small barracks on the outskirts of the city. Saudi Arabia has one of the best anti-terrorist teams in the Middle East, having received training from both the British SAS and the German GSG 9. A preliminary

recce had been carried out by an Arabic-speaking major one month prior to the main team arriving. Both the SAS and the students, all selected from the palace guard, were housed in a barracks on the western edge of the city, close to the old disused Royal Palace grounds. These grounds became the primary training area.

The SAS team used a training programme similar to its own, starting with the basics of weapon training and working up to full practice attacks on both buildings and aircraft. The daily programme was adjusted to accommodate both the mid-day heat and religious prayers. Morning classes would normally start with physical exercises at 05:00 hours, followed by classroom lessons. Breakfast was taken around 09:00 hours, with lunch at 13:00 hours. There would then follow a sleep break until lessons resumed between 17:00 hours and 19:00 hours in the evening. Classroom lessons covered dry weapons training, including instruction in the Browning Hi-Power and the H&K MP5.

Realistic Training

In Week Two range work would begin. Special ranges had been constructed in the desert, both to cover normal close-quarter battle (CQB) shooting and "Killing House" techniques. In the case of the latter, the walls of the building were constructed out of hessian cloth, secured behind a sand bank. Safety was paramount, thus command and control on the ranges required several team members at any one time. The students would progress from basic pistol work, firing double taps, to short, controlled bursts with the MP5.

As the students moved on to the makeshift "Killing House", they were formed into teams, learning the more difficult house-clearing techniques. As previously mentioned, the training area allocated to the SAS was the old palace grounds, which contained about 300 houses of different styles and layouts, scattered among a variety of streets. The entire complex was surrounded by a 3.2m (10ft) wall, which afforded excellent security. This proved to be a major asset in training the Saudi anti-terrorist team, especially in house-clearing and vehicle ambush drills. Given that the SAS was allowed to blow off doors and generally wreck a building before moving on to another, it added a great deal of authenticity to the assaults. Towards the end of the training, with several royal members present, a full-scale exercise was carried out both on the buildings and in the streets.

Aircraft assaults were practised at the airport. At first a military C-130 was used because at the time the Saudi royal household used a converted

C-130 to travel around in. An accident happened during one practice assault on the rear door of the C-130; when the door was opened, an SAS instructor had his thumb completely severed. The thumb was saved by a doctor who sewed it back on. Later the students practised on a Boeing 727, and again a final exercise included an aircraft assault. Less than a year later, the Saudi unit went into operation when a group of fanatics took over the main mosque in Mecca – it did a great job and ended the siege.

Below: The SAS and SBS have trained some of the best counter-terrorist groups in the Far East, such as the Brunei STK unit and specialist formations of the Malaysian armed forces (below).

The SAS has a long-standing relationship with Brunei, which continues to this day. This small but vital country is tucked away in the northwest corner of Borneo, between the Malaysian states of Sarawak and Sabah. A former British protectorate, Brunei's Sheikh Azahari staged a revolt there in 1962. His plan was to become prime minister over what he wanted to be known as North Kalimantan, an area containing Brunei, Sarawak and Sabah. The revolt did not last long, crushed within eight days by British troops brought in from Singapore. The SAS arrived too late to become involved in that particular conflict. However, some of the guerrilla forces that escaped later joined up with the Clandestine Communist Organization (CCO), a group with which the SAS was to become familiar during the jungle campaign fought in Sabah and Kalimantan between 1963 and 1966.

The SAS in Brunei

Today Brunei is a tranquil nation, populated by a warm and friendly people. Most of the 277,000 inhabitants are of Malay origin, but the country is also home to Chinese, Indians and Europeans. Islam is the state religion that co-exists happily with other beliefs, which are openly practised. The SAS and SBS still visit and train with Brunei forces, and students from SAS Selection attend the Jungle Training School at Tutong. Experts from several nations, including instructors from SAS headquarters, staff this school. The six-week training periods take place in March and September, depending on the Selection course attended. In reciprocation the SAS and SBS provide anti-terrorist training for the STK, Brunei's own specialist counter-terrorist team. These are highly trained soldiers specializing mainly in off-shore protection of the oil rigs, a commodity equally as important to Great Britain

as it is to Brunei. Rigid Inflatable Boats (RIBs) are used to transport the team, although larger, more powerful boats are presently on order. STK personnel are also examining the use of sub-skimming vessels, which will allow them to approach the oil rigs unseen.

I recently had the opportunity to advise the STK on various tactics and anti-terrorist equipment. As I watched the men in action I was pleased to see how professional they have become. They are highly motivated, carrying out their drills with precision and speed. I would rate them as one of the best units in the Far East.

Colombian Operations

As part of a US/British effort to combat the huge narcotics industry in Colombia, members of the Regiment have been sent there since the 1980s to train local police anti-narcotics commandos in infiltration skills. The police commandos are taught how to work in long-range patrols in hostile areas, destroy the factories where the drugs are produced, and to either kill or capture the criminals. The SAS would teach basic jungle tactics, plus a few counter-terrorist methods. The training continued until the early 1990s, normally with a full squadron and a section of SBS personnel. The Americans funded a large percentage of the operational equipment supplied to Colombia, but Great Britain also contributed night sights, waterproof equipment, bergens and military clothing. Despite what the media say concerning the role of the SAS in Colombia, the Regiment never carried out any actual operations against the drugs cartels. This was left to the Americans and Colombians.

Right: Two members of the élite German anti-terrorist unit GSG 9. Like the SAS, GSG 9 trains many of the world's counter-terrorist units, and works closely with the SAS.

CHAPTER 8

Specialist Equipment

Specialist anti-terrorist teams require specialist equipment. Aside from their weaponry and clothing, SAS counter-terrorist personnel require hardware that allows them to approach a target silently and close with terrorists as quickly as possible in order to free hostages.

Counter-terrorist equipment comes in all shapes and sizes, such as protective clothing and weaponry. Most modern anti-terrorist equipment, however, is aimed at the delivery and entry stages of any assault. Although personal protection for the individual soldier is very important, speed getting to the incident site and closing with the terrorists are perhaps the most vital factors in mission success. Terrorists have traditionally tried to make it difficult for any assaulting forces to close with them, knowing full well that they would die as a result. The threat to kill hostages or destroy some vital establishment requires that the terrorists have time to carry out such a threat. This threat is reduced in direct response to the access and assault speed of the attacking forces. For example, if there are four terrorists in an incident who at any given moment all present themselves for clean head shots, the snipers could end the episode in one volley. Unfortunately such an opportunity rarely presents itself, added to which terrorists learn very quickly.

Left: SAS anti-terrorist clothing is designed to protect the wearer from enemy bullets, smoke, gas flames and flying debris during a hostage-rescue attempt.

Above: The outer cover of the Assault Body Armour is manu-factured in Arvex SNX 574 flame-resistant fabric. It provides a very high level of protection against fire.

Over the years the response to this has developed into a refined body of delivery and entry techniques. Some teams, such as the SAS, even have dedicated members whose sole purpose during training is to come up with new ways of overcoming obstacles during an assault. Approach and entry methods are roughly divided into covert or overt techniques. Covert entry requires making a silent entry into a terrorist stronghold. This can mean anything from forcing doors or windows open using hydraulic rams and spreaders, to lock-picking. In some cases a small amount of noise is

generated by the entry device, usually countered by the deliberate generation of non-suspicious masking noise. A common procedure is to increase ambient street and traffic noise. During the Iranian Embassy siege in 1980, for example, commercial aircraft flying to Heathrow were re-routed over the terrorist scene, the noise of the flight masking the noise of drilling while inserting surveillance devices in the embassy. Contrived roadworks provide a similar deception. Such noises are acceptable in the right circumstances, particularly in cities and built-up residential areas. The main advantage of a covert entry is that the assault team can be positioned with great precision, ready for the final assault.

Methods of Entry

Overt entry normally means making an entry without any attempt to conceal entry noise. Blowing a hole through a brick wall is a perfect example – there is an explosion rapidly followed by a large hole in the committed wall, plus a cloud of dust. Debris and broken glass from the shock waves add to the equation. The main advantage of an overt entry is that it can disorientate the terrorists by its violence. It also acts as a final commitment by the counter-terrorist unit, i.e. the assault must follow instantly.

Methods of entry are partly dictated by the isolation of the terrorist stronghold and by the available means of delivering the assaulting force. Again, delivery methods are split into covert and overt approaches. Some overt means of approach do not allow for a covert entry, and vice versa. For example, approaching a building using an aggressive vehicle platform delivery system tends to prohibit discreet lock-picking. The correct delivery method must be matched with the best entry technique. Only when this occurs is the assault force able to close and make contact with the enemy in the shortest amount of time. A secondary consideration in assault planning is to ensure that all the assault team gain access to the target area. If the assaulting force is not properly protected during deployment, the opportunity arises for the terrorists to reduce SAS numbers prior to close contact. For example, if the terrorists booby-trap their stronghold, or are presented with clear targets during the assault team's delivery stage, they have an opportunity to deplete the assault force's numbers. Though most anti-terrorist personnel are prepared to accept such a danger, a diminished assault force reduces the chances of a successful mission. The SAS therefore must have the right equipment, a task that rests firmly with the Operations Research Cell.

Above: Anti-Terrorist Team members can wear ceramic plates for extra protection against high-velocity bullets, including armour-piercing rounds.

Right: The Assault Body Armour is designed to accommodate the CT500 Radio Communications Harness to keep open team communications during an assault.

The Operations Research Cell is usually manned by two long-serving SAS soldiers, normally holding the rank of sergeant or corporal. They are tasked with finding or developing the specialized equipment the Regiment requires for its operational roles. This equipment can range from weapons, clothing and vehicles, to food and radios. Any SAS soldier may approach Ops Research and request information on a product or put forward an idea for development. When the Anti-Terrorist Team was formed, Ops Research was requested to find a device that would disorientate a terrorist without harming any hostages within close proximity. They in turn asked the technical experts at Royal Enfield to help. Several devices were made, but of these the most popular was the Stun Grenade. Other devices such as the "Screamer" were also developed. The Screamer would emit a very loud, high-pitched scream. However, though it disorientated the terrorists, it was also capable of deafening the hostages and the SAS assault team.

Those soldiers employed in Ops Research are not dissimilar to "Q" in the James Bond movies. Over the years they have developed some quite brilliant equipment, from motorized parachutes to space-age crossbows capable of penetrating 1.3cm (0.5in) of metal at 100m (305ft). This chapter examines some of the ingenious equipment invented or used by the SAS in the course of anti-terrorist operations.

Personal Body Armour

Standard SAS body armour is designated Assault Body Armour. Available in differing grades of ballistic protection, according to clients' operational requirements, it can incorporate a groin protector and pockets in front and rear for the insertion of

Left: *Anti-terrorist personnel often clip magazines together to facilitate quick reload times. During an assault a target will receive sustained fire until he or she is knocked to the ground.*

be fitted with a radio pouch and magazine carriers or utility pouches if so required. Level III Plus ceramic plates provide protection against high-velocity bullets up to and including 7.62mm x 51 US M61 Ball Armour Piercing and 7.62mm x 54 Soviet Heavy Ball (Steel Core) ammunition when worn with body armour. Weighing 2.5kg (5.5lb) and measuring 250 x 300mm (9.8 x 11.8in), the plate can be worn in the front and rear of the Assault Body Armour.

Assault Belt Rig

The assault belt rig was originally designed for the SAS Anti-Terrorist Team. It houses the soldier's personal weapons, ammunition and grenades. Manufactured in top-quality black bridle leather, it comprises a heavy duty fully lined belt, a pistol holster and two magazine carriers, a grenade carrier holding two stun grenades, and a three-magazine carrier for the MP5 submachine gun. Canvas versions of the same style rig are also used. Where the assault member is required to carry a lot of equipment, a load-bearing vest with multiple pockets can be worn.

Lock-picking fascinates many people as it facilitates a secret way into other people's property. The SAS first started using lock-picking techniques while working in Northern Ireland and some members became experts in the field. Lock-picking is used when a covert entry is vital. Though the principles seem fairly elementary, lock-picking is a skilful art that takes many years to learn properly. These skills require constant practice to achieve what is known as the "feel The feel is acquired through a combination of touch and an imaginary portrayal of what the picks are doing inside the lock. A lock can only be opened by a key or by mimicking the actions of that key. The SAS has access to a wide range of individual lock-picking sets, and fairly ingenious

Above: Like firemen, SAS counter-terrorist soldiers may wear oxygen-breathing equipment if entering a highly toxic environment. Such kit is bulky, though.

protective ceramic plates. A ballistic collar can be fitted if required. The outer cover of the Assault Body Armour is manufactured in Arvex SNX 574 flame-resistant fabric. Based on Nomex Delta C fibre and with a weight of 210 grams (7.35oz) per square metre, this fabric is also anti-static and liquid repellent. It provides a very high level of protection against fire and burning liquids. The Assault Body Armour is designed to accommodate the CT500 Radio Communications Harness and can

Above: The latest version of the Heckler & Koch G3 assault rifle. Rugged, accurate and extremely reliable, the G3 has been in use with the SAS for many years.

Below: The SIG P226 semi-automatic pistol. This Swiss weapon is now replacing the Hi-Power as the SAS's main pistol. The P226 is one of the most reliable pistols in the world.

devices known as lock-picking guns. These are basically mechanically driven lock-picks that help speed up the process of getting a lock open.

Weaponry

It is worth giving Heckler & Koch a special mention as their weaponry has done much to aid anti-terrorist teams worldwide. Three former Mauser employees founded Heckler & Koch in 1947. The company had its first big break when, in 1959, the West German Army adopted its G3 assault rifle. The MP5 was developed from the successful G3 rifle and shares many similar characteristics. Unlike most other submachine guns, the MP5 fires from a closed and locked bolt, using the same delayed-blowback action as the G3. This makes the weapon expensive to produce, but the increased safety and accuracy compensate for this. Heckler & Koch now have factories worldwide, its weapons being used in over 50 countries.

Heckler & Koch MP5

Specification: Calibre: 9 x 19mm Parabellum; Weight: 2.55kg (5.62lb); Muzzle velocity: 400mps (1219fps); Magazine capacity: 15- or 30-round box.

Below: *The middle two weapons are MP5 submachine guns (the other two are Russian AKs). The MP5 is used by the SAS Anti-Terrorist Team and just about every other counter-terrorist unit.*

Below: *Modern crossbows are lightweight, silent, have good range and their composite bolts can go through wood and even metal. Crossbows are excellent for short-range silent killing.*

The MP5 is the weapon of choice for many of the world's anti-terrorist units, including the SAS. It was the weapon used by the Regiment during the Iranian Embassy siege. Its closed-bolt mechanism makes it the most accurate submachine gun currently on the market. There are various versions of the MP5, including one with a telescopic metal stock and another with a short barrel.

SIG Sauer P226

Specification: Calibre: 9 x 19mm Parabellum; Weight: 0.75kg (1.65lbs); Muzzle Velocity: 350mps (1067fps); Magazine capacity: 15- or 20-round box.

Developed by SIG in the 1980s, the P226 combines features from the P220 and P225 models. Costly but effective, it passed every required specification in the US joint services pistol trials. One of the best performers in the pistol world, it is replacing the Browning Hi-Power within the SAS.

Heckler & Koch G3

Specification: Calibre: 7.62 x 51mm NATO; Weight: 4.40kg (9.7lb); Magazine: 20-round box; Muzzle velocity: 790mps (2408fps).

The Gewehr 3 has its origins in a Mauser design which curiously found its way through Spain, Holland and eventually back to Germany, where Heckler & Koch took on the task of perfecting the G3 into the weapon we know today.

The weapon is robust and reliable, which is why so many armies around the world have chosen it as their standard infantry weapon. The G3/SG1 sniper weapon comes with a telescopic sight and bipod and has an adjustable hair-trigger. The SAS uses the SG1 for the snipers on the Anti-Terrorist Team. It is a very reliable weapon.

Accuracy International L96A1 PM Sniper Rifle

Specification: Calibre: 7.62 x 51mm NATO Match; Weight: 6.5kg (14.3lb) with sight; Muzzle velocity: 850mps (2591fps); Magazine capacity: 10-round box.

The current favoured sniper rifle of the SAS. The PM is designed and manufactured by Accuracy International and has a reputation for great accuracy in any conditions, giving head shots at a range of up to 600m (1829ft).

The rifle can be fitted with different sights according to what is required. There are also various versions of the model, including one that can be used in Arctic conditions without freezing up. The PM is a bolt-action rifle with a stainless-steel barrel.

The rifle is very comfortable to fire and the head need not be moved during bolt operation, allowing

Below: *This is the Five-Seven pistol produced by Browning. A development of the Hi-Power, it is a worthy competitor of the P226 for the Regiment's favours.*

for continuous observation. It has a bipod and a retractable spike on the rear of the butt. It is also available in a covert model which is suppressed, and a Super Magnum version which fires either .338 Lapua Magnum, .300 Winchester Magnum or 7mm Remington Magnum rounds.

Laser Rangefinder

Specification: Weight: 2.2kg (1lb); Range: 10km (6.2 miles); Field width: 7 degrees; Magnification: x 7.

The laser rangefinder is about the size of a pair of 7 x 50 binoculars. It gives the range of a target accurate to within 5m (15ft) up to a range of 10km (6.2 miles). The SAS and British armed forces use the SIMRAD LP7 to provide an accurate range for direct-fire weapons. The rangefinder is particularly

effective for Mortar Fire Controllers (MFCs) or artillery Forward Observation Officers (FOOs). The range is displayed in the eyepiece and there is an indicator to denote if more than one target has been detected. A minimum-range control cuts out unwanted reflections. The LP7 has a times seven magnification and is combined with an optical receiver, which allows a four-digit LED display to be observed through the left eyepiece, superimposed on the picture seen in the right eyepiece.

Remington 870 Combat Shotgun

Specification: Pump-action; Calibre: 12 gauge 70mm (2.75in); Weight: 3.6kg (7.9lb); Ammunition types: buckshot, birdshot, solid slug, flechette, CS, plastic baton and many others; Magazine capacity: seven-round tubular.

The Remington is one of the most widely manufactured shotguns in the world, and is currently the standard US Marine shotgun. Its pump action and the variety of ammunition available make it ideal for counter-terrorist and security work. Combined with the Hatton round, the SAS uses it for shooting doors off their hinges.

Above: Abseiling is a skill taught to all members of the Anti-Terrorist Team. Abseiling is one of the main delivery methods used during a hostage-rescue operation.

Left: The Heckler & Koch MP5K is the shortened version of the MP5 submachine gun. The MP5K has a cyclic rate of fire of 900 rounds per minute.

Below: Rubber-soled assault boots are an essential part of the anti-terrorist soldier's kit. It is imperative that assault teams do not slip during a rescue.

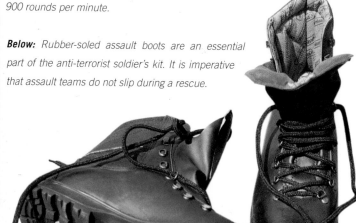

Rip Ammunition

Rip ammunition is specially designed to dislodge a door. It is fired from a shotgun, with the user placing the muzzle directly at the door hinge or lock.

A well-practised assault-team member can fire four shots, removing all three hinges and the lock in under three seconds. The cartridges contain micronized CS, insertion powder and non-toxic powder, which in turn produce carbon dioxide. When the gun muzzle is held against a wooden door, it will blast a hole through a thickness of up to 65mm (2.6in). Impact disperses the irritant, which forms an incapacitating cloud large enough to fill a room 3 x 3m (9 x 9ft) in size and render it a no-go, no-stay area. Rip ammunition can also be used to penetrate vehicle windows up to a range of 3m (9ft), and 12mm (0.4in) Makralon armoured glass at 1.5m (4.5ft).

Arwen

The Arwen is a 37mm gas-, smoke- and baton-round launcher. It is essentially an anti-riot weapon adapted for hostage-rescue. It has a five-round rotating magazine which works in a similar way to the cylinder on a revolver. The baton round will cause immobilizing damage up to 100m (304ft), although the accuracy is limited. The CS gas rounds vary; some are capable of penetrating light wooden doors and glass before discharging.

Delivery Systems

The Fast Rope Insertion/Extraction System (FRIES) is basically a rope manufactured from high-tensile multifilament nylon, with eight nylon rope loops incorporated in the last few metres. FRIES enables anti-terrorist personnel to be deployed into, and retrieved from, dangerous situations simply by clipping themselves and their equipment to the loops with quick-release karabiners. The system increases deployment speed of airborne forces and reduces the risk to aircraft and personnel. A Blackhawk helicopter using a two-rope system is capable of delivering a group of 12 men in a little over 10 seconds once in the correct hover. The rope is suspended from a helicopter, enabling the soldiers to attach themselves. The system is

Right: With ships and oil rigs being potential terrorist targets, sub-surface vessels have been developed as a delivery method. They allow assault teams to approach targets unseen.

aircraft consisted of a three-wheeler trike and a ram-air parachute.

The trike had a rear-mounted engine with the propeller housed in a protective cage. The pilot would be strapped into an open seat in front of the engine, where his right foot would control the accelerator. Revving the engine would speed the trike forward, forcing the ram-air parachute that was attached to the trike to act as a wing. The Microlight had very short take-off and landing distances, added to which a pilot could be taught to fly it in less than a day.

Despite the fact that it was almost impossible to stall the Microlight, SAS trials were discontinued after several messy landings. Backpack-mounted Para Hawks were also trialed, and while these were taken up by other countries the SAS did not envisage a requirement. The new version Para Hawks manufactured in the US are much improved and the SAS are evaluating their potential.

Above: Ladder and platform systems capable of carrying up to 12 men per vehicle reduce assault and access times.

designed to be non-rotating to enable problem-free deployment. It also has a high-extension capability which absorbs dynamic loads. This facilitates smoother physical sensations when troops need to be "snatched" out quickly.

Para Hawk

The Para Hawk is a propeller-powered platform which uses a parachute as a "wing". Although it was first developed in the US, the idea was taken up by a retired SAS pilot who started designing his own aircraft in Hereford.

The first models were ready around the mid-1980s, and the SAS carried out field trials on the Microlight aircraft, as it was then known. The

Convertible High-Speed Surface/Submarine Vessel

This is a fast offshore boat which has deflatable / re-inflatable hull tubes and waterproofed, pressurized operating systems. While on the surface it serves as an offshore rigid hull, which can be converted into mini-submarine mode in less than 20 seconds, even while sailing.

The boat is powered by outboard motors on the surface and electric propulsion underwater. It is capable of carrying up to six combat divers plus equipment, together with standard fuel bags.

Surface range is 185km (100 nautical miles) at over 54km/h (30 knots), while underwater it has a range of 10km (5.39 nautical miles) at around 3.7–7km/h (2–3 knots). It can dive to 100m (304ft).

The underwater performance is greatly improved by substituting standard lead-acid batteries with silver-zinc units. The boats can be deployed from a road trailer towed by a large car, from a submarine, a patrol craft or by helicopter, the deployment method affecting the combat diver's range and operational capabilities. Sub-skimmer craft are uniquely versatile, making them indispensable for reconnaissance, surveillance, agent handling in hostile territorial waters and waterborne clandestine missions where divers are involved. They offer an ideal method of covert approach for such scenarios as oil-rig and ship-at-sea assault operations.

Abseiling

The SAS uses abseiling in two main ways: descending a rock face during mountain training or operations, and as an entry method in anti-terrorist work. The abseil harness is designed to be used as a

full-body harness, permitting a team member to be suspended for protracted periods of time (i.e. outside a window). This item comprises a waist-belt harness and a chest harness connected by a combi-sling.

Abseil ropes are 11mm (0.4in) in diameter, non-stretch, black polyester rope. They are available in differing pre-cut lengths of 50m (152ft), 100m (304ft), 150m (457ft) and 200m (609ft).

Various descenders are used. The ANKA descender is a horned figure "8" abseil descender with the lower ring set at 90 degrees to the upper one, eliminating any tendency to twist during a descent. The STOP descender works on the "fail safe" principle, which requires the user to apply

Below: Abseiling harnesses allow SAS troopers to rapidly and safely exit from helicopters during an assault. The ropes pass through special descenders that prevent snagging.

Right: Blowing holes in walls is often essential during hostage-rescue attempts. The main problems associated with such actions are flying debris and the danger of injuring hostages.

Above: A way of getting around the problem of using explosives to blow holes through walls is the Wall-Breaching Cannon, currently in use with the SAS.

pressure on its handle for the rope to move through it. Release of the handle causes descent to be halted immediately. Karabiners, fitted with locking screwgates and having a breaking strain of 3000kg (6123lb), join the separate abseiling units. Rope bags are used during anti-terrorist work to facilitate smooth deployment of a rope during a descent.

Vehicle Ladder and Platform Systems

The most common delivery system used by most anti-terrorist teams today is a vehicle ladder and platform system. The system provides the assault team with both delivery and access to buildings, trains, coaches and aircraft. While a covert assault may dictate the use of normal assault ladders, both the Immediate Action (IA) and a rapid assault are best carried out by the employment of a vehicle-mounted multi-role personnel delivery system.

There are various systems being developed. Some are designed to fit permanently onto armoured vehicles, while other systems are carried within a standard pick-up truck and can be assembled in minutes. In both cases the

Above: The Wall-Breaching Cannon is a brilliant invention that does away with the use of explosives. It fires a jet of water that knocks a hole through a wall but then immediately dissipates.

assembled ladders are configured to suit a wide range of user needs. They are capable of deploying fully equipped personnel to a variety of structural levels. For example, the system can be adjusted to deliver a 10-man assault team directly to the doors of a Boeing 747. The same system can be adjusted in a few minutes to assault a building window some 7m (21ft) above ground level.

The system is also valid for assaulting ships when in dock. The assault team members are carried on load-carrying platforms secured to the sides, top and front hood of the vehicle. In addition to this, ladders can be formed into access bridges when a gap needs to be crossed. It is also possible to fit a 360-degree turntable with

an extended ladder similar to that used by fire fighters. This arrangement facilitates multi-role functions at difficult angles.

Assault Systems

Ladders were one of the first items of equipment utilized by the SAS when the team was formed. Today the SAS uses an extensive range of assault ladders of differing widths, which cater for the majority of operational requirements during a siege situation.

Ladder types include single section, multi-section and extending types in single-width, double-width and triple-stile designs. All ladders are manufactured from structural-grade aluminium

Below: The Wall-Breaching Cannon in action. There is no back-blast when using this device, unlike with conventional explosives, which means a more rapid entry.

Above: The great advantage with vehicle ladder and platform systems is that they can be adjusted to reach any aircraft door or building window. This increases assault speed.

alloy with deeply serrated rung sections and heavy duty rectangular sections.

They are built to SAS order and thus non-standard designs and lengths are available. All ladders are fitted as standard with non-slip rubber feet, noise-reducing buffers on all exposed faces, and are finished in a black polyester powder coating.

Single Section Ladders

These ladders are available to the SAS in single and double widths and triple-stile designs up to 4m (12ft) in length. They offer silent climbing and are ideally suited for gaining rapid access to public transport vehicles, ships, aircraft, or for scaling walls. Wall hooks and sniper platforms can be fitted to all sizes.

Multi-Sectional Ladders

Manufactured mainly in double-width or triple-stile configurations, these ladders range in length

Above: Crowbars may be unsophisticated, but if they get the job done they are as effective as any other item in the Special Air Service's armoury.

from 1m (3ft) up to 4m (12ft) and can be quickly assembled to give finished lengths of up to 8m (24ft). They are transported easily in vans or estate cars and provide team capability for two to four personnel, depending on length and conditions on the ground. They are fitted as standard with heavy duty channel connectors

Frame Charge/Flexible Cutting Charge

The frame charge was originally a wooden frame to which metal-cased explosive was attached, with the aim of blowing a hole through a wall.

The size of the frame depended on the area which was to be blown, and the amount of explosive depended on the thickness of the wall.

The early frame charge has since been developed by Royal Ordnance into a cutting explosive known as Blade. This is a linear-shaped charge made from DEMIEX 200: an EDX-based plastic explosive which detonates in excess of 8200mps (25,000fps). Internally, copper produces a shaped-charge jet which, on initiation by an L2A1/L1A1 detonator, cuts with fine precision. Blade is fitted with a self-adhesive strip for attachment to the target.

The charge is covered by a sheath of close-cell foam. Blade comes in five different weights and thicknesses, each of which can be cut with a knife and tailored to the task.

Blade can be incorporated into a conventional explosive ring-main with charges linked together with detonating cord for simultaneous detonation. Developing the frame charge was an interesting experiment, as the SAS has a tendency to add more explosive than is necessary. During several early experiments the frame charges were known to knock down a whole house, instead of just making a hole in the wall.

The value of frame charges was clearly illustrated during the Iranian Embassy siege in London, when the front assault team attached one to the French windows. Although still available, frame charges have been superseded by the less lethal Wall-Breaching Cannon.

The Wall-Breaching Cannon is a device that eliminates the need for using high-explosives as a method of entry in a hostage situation.

Every wall differs and it is very difficult to judge the amount of explosive required to blow a hole

complete with nylon slides and locking pins. Sniper platforms are also available for use with these ladders.

Extension Ladders (Multi-Level)

These give the SAS a choice of widths, including triple stile, with single and double sliding sections available. Standard fittings include full-length nylon slides, quadruple-section restraining brackets, over-extension stops and an auto-swing safety clutch.

without causing a mass of flying debris on the opposite side. The debris can obviously cause indiscriminate injury to foes and hostages.

The SAS has no second chance during any assault, therefore for walls of unknown strength more explosive than necessary is invariably used, compounding the undesired lethal debris effects. The Wall-Breaching Cannon is a more suitable alternative to using high-explosives.

Wall breaching in a hostage situation involves the following requirements: the device has to be instantaneous, it must pose minimal threat to hostages and the assaulting team, it must cause only minimal damage to walls, and the assault team must be able to act at the moment of breaching.

Below: Sometimes SAS counter-terrorist soldiers do not need to enter a building – a target can be neutralized from the outside if the opportunity presents itself.

To this end the Wall-Breaching Cannon, also known as the "Harvey Wallbanger", was developed. It is designed to direct a heavy, soft projectile with sufficient kinetic energy to breach a wall, then instantly dissipate the energy after breaching.

A water-filled plastic container fired by compressed air fills this requirement very adequately. The container is launched from a muzzle-loaded, smoothbore barrel. The rear of the barrel is fitted with an air reservoir separated from the main barrel by an entrapped glass disc, which ruptures by electrical detonation at a given pressure, thus presenting instantaneous pressure to the rear of the projectile. A loose piston stops any air leakage past the projectile, giving good velocity

Left: *The SAS has experimented with suction pads.*

Below: *Sledgehammers were used at the Iranian Embassy siege.*

Above: Not everything the SAS uses is hi-tech. These men, for example, have commercially available torches attached to their MP5 submachine guns.

at pressures between 200, 400 and 600psi. The system can be transported along with 10 x 23-litre (5-gallon) plastic containers in both helicopters or vehicles with ease. A two-man team can carry it and it can pass through any standard doorway.

Rapid Entry Equipment

The SAS has a wide range of equipment designed to enable rapid entry through doors, windows and walls of buildings. The equipment is normally known as "brute force equipment", and includes everything from a sledgehammer to cutting equipment similar to that used by fire and rescue crews.

The back-up truck which supports the Anti-Terrorist Team carries with it a full and comprehensive range of silent hydraulic cutters and spreaders, as well as a range of rams, crowbars and axes. These include the following:

1. Manual Door Ram: a hand-held ram designed to force open inward-opening doors by being swung against the lock area and imparting a weight load of approximately three tons. It is effective against all but reinforced steel doors. Weight: 16kg (35lb).

2. Door Ripper: a lightweight tool designed to force outward-opening doors with the blade being driven between door and frame in the area of the lock. A ratchet mechanism allows the blade to be worked behind the door to provide increased force.

3. Hydraulic Door Ram: designed to force reinforced inward-opening doors. Supplied with

Above: Rapid-entry equipment includes claw hammers and bolt cutters – anything that can facilitate the Anti-Terrorist Team getting close to the terrorists before they kill their hostages.

three sets of claws to suit all standard widths of door from 760mm (30in) to 920mm (36in).

The main ram is positioned over the lock area while the secondary ram forces the jaws into the frame. Operation of a valve activates the main ram to force the door open with a maximum force of five tons. An 11-ton version is also available.

Extending Pole and Hook

This marine assault access system has been designed to provide anti-terrorist personnel with the means of entry into elevated marine structures and vessels from the water.

The system, which raises a flexible ladder and grapple, is particularly suitable where silence and

stealth are of paramount importance. The device is compact, extremely portable and has proven operational advantages unsurpassed by any other existing equipment. One diver easily deploys the device to the target, and its compact design allows mobilization within seconds and easy manoeuvrability during operation. The system is used by both the SAS and SBS, where quick access is required and traditional ladder or grappling hook systems are not feasible.

Suction Pads

This unique system incorporates four vacuum pads (one for each hand and foot) and allows the individual to climb almost any flat surface. Each pad is controlled with a small computer unit. This constantly measures and adjusts the vacuum force of each pad. A visual and acoustic warning signal informs the user about the load-carrying capacity of each pad. There is a fail-safe method which ensures only one pad can be removed at any time. The climbing process is accomplished by the operator pulling slightly upwards on the pad to release it. The pads will automatically adhere to almost any surface including concrete, sandstone, plaster, wood, glass and metal.

The unit is operated using compressed air, which is supplied by an air cylinder worn on the back of the operator. Each cylinder lasts up to two hours. Apart from this there is no external energy source.

Below: Sophisticated cutting devices in use with British emergency services are also used by the SAS to cut through metal obstacles.

The total unit weight is about 25kg (55lb), yet the system allows for a carrying capacity of almost 1000kg (2200lb). Training time is minimal and most operators are able to climb a vertical surface after only 30 minutes. Overhangs and concave climbs can also be circumnavigated.

The system is new and as yet untested in the anti-terrorist role, however its potential is promising. Analysis indicates that shipping is one of the avenues open to terrorism, and in the event access methods such as this will prove invaluable.

Thermal Lance

The thermal lance is designed for cutting mild steel, and is capable of operating underwater. The basic system consists of a 4m (12ft) flexible thermal lance made from Kerie cable, a single 3-litre (5-pint) oxygen cylinder fitted with pressure gauges, a pressure regulator, a battery powered igniter and a three-way valve which switches the system's working pressure on or off. Once ignited, the Kerie cable burns at approximately 0.6m (2ft) a minute during cutting, which gives a maximum cutting time of six minutes.

The SAS Anti-Terrorist Team carries a backpack-portable system that weighs 10.5kg (23lb), which is used for cutting during assault entry. It is generally used in covert entry assaults – although it burns very bright it is fairly silent.

Grapnel Launcher

This device is very similar to those used by the military for assaulting cliff faces. The current version favoured by the SAS Anti-Terrorist Team is shoulder launched. It fires a grapple hook to a height of 75m (228ft). The attached rope is then climbed by the assault team members.

Although it has its uses, the problem with the grapnel launcher is its loud percussion on firing and the time it takes to climb the rope. However, they have been found suitable for accessing ships and oil rigs.

One simple method of getting into a car quietly is to use a strip of plastic banding. This needs to be folded in two, with the loop end forced though the rubber seal around the door. Due to the nature of the tape the plastic strip can be slid down and manipulated to fit over the door button release. Once the button is trapped, the plastic strip can be manoeuvred upwards carefully to open the door silently.

The same approach can be used to retrieve keys left in the lock on the inside of a door, and to open house windows secured by ram and pin security measures.

The SAS has access to a properly manufactured version of the plastic band, which is far more effective and guarantees access into 80 percent of all vehicles. It leaves little or no damage to the vehicle when used to gain access, and thus is ideal when entering a vehicle to fit a covert surveillance device, such as a video camera or microphone. The same device can also be used to re-lock the vehicle.

It is difficult for divers to communicate underwater without the use of an umbilical line. However, a new system has emerged for such a

task. The diver speaks into a mask, or mouthpiece-mounted microphone (various microphone and earphone configurations are possible to fit a range of masks and breathing systems). Such is the range of equipment available to the SAS.

Below: *SAS divers are currently equipped with mouthpiece-mounted microphones that allow individual members of underwater teams to communicate with each other.*

CHAPTER 9

The Future

The attacks on the World Trade Center in September 2001 ushered in a new era of terrorism. Notwithstanding the many anti-terrorist units and intelligence agencies in the West, terrorists have access to bio-chemical weapons and the will to use them.

Until 11 September 2001, I would have said that members of the SAS Anti-Terrorist Team were well equipped and able to counter any terrorist incident. However, since the attacks on the United States this state of readiness has to be re-evaluated. Whilst my trust in the individual SAS soldier is not in question, the capabilities of the enemy and his methods of attack have increased. How we defend ourselves against terrorism in the future is governed to some degree by what we have learnt from the past. We have fought modern-day terrorism since the early 1960s. Some battles we have won, some we have lost. In either case we have become wiser, adjusting our planning and counter-measures to combat the tactics of the various terrorist organizations. Much will depend on what direction future terrorist attacks take. We would be fools to bury our heads in the sand and say that 11 September was a one-off. We must face up to the possible means and targets open to

Left: An oil refinery is a choice target for terrorists. A hijacked aircraft can be crashed into it by terrorists seeking martyrdom, causing widespread death and destruction.

terrorist organizations and confront them with realistic counter-measures.

Political rhetoric is always at the front end of any terrorist attack, with politicians and world leaders condemning all such atrocities. Unfortunately much of this falls short of any real action. For example, the British Government announced on 1 March 2001 that it intended to ban active support in Great Britain for many international terrorist organizations under its new anti-terrorist legislation. The list of organizations included 21 terrorist groups, such as the Basque separatist organization ETA, the Kurdish PKK based in Turkey, and the Tamil Tiger guerrillas in Sri Lanka. Also on the list was the *Al Qaeda* network of Osama bin Laden. Despite the legislation, ETA still carried out assassinations, the PPK killed by car bomb, and Osama bin Laden ordered the attacks on the US. The legislation was the British Parliament's response to criticism from governments abroad, including the United States, that the UK was "a haven for terror organizations". True, the law makes it illegal to encourage terrorist activities abroad, and anyone who openly supports a banned organization, either verbally or via fund-raising, can be arrested. Realistically, however, political criticism carries little weight with terrorist organizations. How do we stop them?

Stopping the Terrorists

Without doubt this is the big question being asked today, and it will remain the key issue for many years to come. The reaction to the attacks on America was one of unity, as the world community gathered in condemnation of the terrorist onslaught. Such unity may be short-lived, though. Many Western nations may stay the course, but there are those countries which openly oppose the US. My father had a saying: "No matter how good you think you are, someone always thinks you're a

bastard." In a similar vein, the news that America had been attacked was well received in some countries. Pictures of men, women and children dancing joyfully in the streets in the Middle East were all over the television channels, though it would be fair to say that these countries and their peoples, such as Syria, had grievances against the US. In retaliation, many Muslims living in the West were attacked, some people were even stopped from boarding passenger aircraft because they simply looked Muslim. I have spent, and still spend, much of my life working with Muslim people both in the Middle and Far East. Each Muslim nation is as diverse as nations are in the West, and their peoples warrant individual assessment, not blanket judgement.

Understanding Islam

For the Muslim nations social tolerance is governed mainly by religion. A few examples will suffice. You steal, I will cut off your hand. You commit adultery, and I will stone you to death. Such laws are something Western nations see as barbaric. On the other hand, many Muslim believers see Christian nations as decadent, openly exhibiting sex, drugs and lewd behaviour. In truth both sides are correct. What really matters is how much tolerance we allow each other. Wealth also plays a major part in a nation's character. Money conveys power and respect in all walks of life. In turn, many of the poorer nations look on the richer countries with envy. For many terrorist organizations this is one of the factors that fuels their aggression. As long as the nations of the earth have differing religious beliefs and variations in wealth, we will

Left: The twin towers of New York's World Trade Center, which were destroyed during terrorist attacks orchestrated by the Saudi terrorist Osama bin Laden on 11 September 2001.

Above: Air traffic control centres are vulnerable to terrorist attacks, but not in the traditional sense. A terrorist operator could cause widespread destruction sitting at a console.

always have terrorism. A look at the list of main terrorist organizations and what they represent will confirm this.

Ask any adult and they will tell you exactly where they were on 11 September 2001. Personally I was asleep, having my afternoon siesta, which is common in Spain. I awoke to shouts of "come and look at this". Two hours later, several of our friends arrived and we spent the rest of the day discussing the terrible incident as it continued to unfold before our eyes. The magnitude of the attack made it look like a movie, there was even live footage of the second aircraft actually crashing into the World Trade Center. Having spent my life fighting or writing about terrorism, I sat mesmerized as the dramatic scenes were played and relived repeatedly by the world's media.

The most gruelling scene for me was the sight of people throwing themselves from the windows – no one should be faced with that decision and I can not imagine what inner strength it must have taken to commit such an act. We were entering a new phase in the terrorist war. Above all, I recognized that the terrorists' principles had changed. In the past they had always used a hijacked aircraft to enforce a set of demands, using the lives of the passengers and crew as bargaining chips. Now they had hijacked several aircraft and transformed them into flying bombs. The flying bombs really had no use for the passengers, other than being a deterrent stopping the authorities shooting down the aircraft. What worried me more was the use of the "martyr" as a terrorist weapon.

Left: *The most vulnerable place on an aircraft is the flight deck. If hijackers seize an aircraft they have in effect a flying bomb which they can crash into choice targets (above).*

Smart bombs, laser-guided missiles, multi-million dollar fighter aircraft and a defence budget running into billions cannot stop what has become the most powerful weapon in the terrorist arsenal. It offers a perfect guidance system with full stealth facilities. When in range it can identify its target with 100 percent accuracy. If threatened, it can abort and go immediately to a secondary target without being re-programmed. Its lethality is unlimited and thousands more become available every day. In its basic form, the martyr simply straps a huge amount of explosives around his or her body and walks to a place where the enemy is located. At the right moment he or she detonates the explosives, killing himself and all those in the immediate vicinity. This type of martyr is normally used against civilian

targets. A more advanced martyr uses a larger amount of explosives in a car or a truck. This type of martyr is normally reserved for military or government installations, where a degree of resistance is offered. The car or truck is then rammed into the weakest point before being detonated.

The new, more specialized martyr is highly intelligent. It spends months, even years, working on its operation, utilizing the full expanse of its intelligence before choosing a target. This martyr seizes an aircraft and flies it into a building with devastating effectiveness. So what next and when will they strike? They will learn from the past and they will wait, remaining dormant until their enemy has once more begun to relax its vigilance. In the interim they will plan and make new preparations. It is estimated that over 3000 people died as a result of the attacks on the World Trade Center. Whatever they do next will be equally atrocious. There are lots of targets for them to choose from.

How do we make commercial passenger flying more secure? Back in 1960 sky marshals were introduced after a series of hijackings in the Middle East. They are still used today, especially with such airlines as Israel's El Al. Sky marshals are a two-edged weapon. If they are professional, by which I mean they perform as one of the passengers, sitting in a dominating seat with a concealed weapon ready at hand, then I am personally in favour of them. Unfortunately, cost is a factor and many airlines ended up employing armed men who really have no idea about how to exercise their duties with any sense of rationality. I once travelled on a Middle Eastern airliner which employed a sky marshal. He spent most of his time walking up and down the isle frowning at the passengers, showing his hardware and fraternizing with the stewardesses. I could have

taken him out with a catapult and then used his gun to hijack the aircraft.

Aircraft hijacked for the purpose of flying bombs in the future are likely to be shot down before they reach their target; governments will have no other choice. In such circumstances passengers may well try to overpower the hijackers, knowing that if they do not succeed then they are dead anyway. The optimum compromise would be to introduce stricter passenger control and identification. To some degree this has already been done, but how far do the authorities go before the paying passenger says enough is enough and refuses to fly? Another answer is to make it harder to gain

Below: Light aircraft can also be used as flying bombs, or as delivery systems for the distribution of chemical and biological weapons over population centres.

access to the flight deck. That means no one enters during the flight. A camera outside the door could also be mounted to watch over the aisle. The crew could also be given small-arms training and be equipped with a gun. This would at least negate the chance of the aircraft being flown by a martyr.

Cities offer the terrorist the best opportunity for mass destruction, mainly because of the density of population. Almost all major cities in the Western world have a main airport nearby, in some cases the airports are actually in the city. Conversely, any attack does not necessarily have to come from a hijacked aircraft – the most popular option to date is the car bomb. What can we do to protect

the cities? From a hijacked airliner converted into a flying bomb, very little. Once it's over the city shooting it down only serves to guarantee the attack. But buildings have been designed to withstand high winds, earthquakes and floods, so why not terrorist attacks? We need to design buildings that will protect people from terrorist bombs. There needs to be research into why buildings collapse and why there are so many fatalities. We also need building designs that will help prevent injuries from blast debris.

As for a silent biological or chemical attack, the best we can do is inform people of the risks, what to look for and how to prepare themselves in the event of an attack. We need to develop quicker methods for detecting chemical and biological warfare agents in all forms, including in food and water. People need some form of collective

Below: Nuclear power stations are exposed to hijacked aircraft, though any destruction would be limited as they are for the most part situated in isolated areas.

protection against a bio-chemical attack, and there needs to be a better programme of mass decontamination, one suitable for civilians rather than the military. We need to look at every avenue of attack the terrorists might take. For example, water supplies can be used to poison the population. What is needed is some form of system that monitors the water and its supply, giving us a warning of contamination and estimating the population areas most at risk. Such a system is already operational in Salt Lake City and Utah.

Nuclear Reactors

One cannot predict the effects of a commercial aircraft crashing into a nuclear reactor, but a minimum estimate must be 2000 fatalities. There would be a massive explosion, but a nuclear blast is unlikely. However, there would almost certainly be radiation leaks and fallout. Such a crash may even cause a Chernobyl-type melt-down. How we can stop such an event ever happening is problematic. If the countries that build nuclear power stations placed anti-aircraft batteries around the sites, there is the possibility that they would identify and shoot down the aircraft before it impacted, or the aircraft might be intercepted by local air force fighters.

But it is not just from the air that the threat comes. Almost every major city in the world is located on the banks of a river or on the coast. For example, the centre of London can be accessed directly from the River Thames. Oil tankers and container ships continually link cities, nations and continents. Many of these ships are crewed by workers from the Philippines (the world's biggest

Above: It is almost impossible to prevent terrorist attacks upon shipping, or to inspect every ship that docks in port. In addition, small vessels can be packed with explosives to ram larger ones.

Left: The delivery of biological weapons by terrorists is a real concern. The delivery of these weapons is hard to detect, which means the West must have proper defence measures.

crew supplier), which incidentally is also home to the *Abu Sayyaf* militant group. Indonesia (the world's second-biggest crew supplier) is home to numerous radical Muslim groups. In addition, a meagre two percent of shipping containers entering the US are inspected and a container can hold a lot of explosives. Conversely, what if several small, motor-powered launches or light aircraft packed with high-explosives were to ram important shipping (remember the Kamikaze pilots of World War II)? If the target was a holiday cruise liner the attack would cause thousands of deaths. If they attacked oil tankers then the revenue lost and the ecological damage would be

Above: Innocent crop-sprayers can be turned into deadly bio-chemical weapons dispensers with very little effort. This is the nightmare scenario that now threatens the West.

horrendous. If several vessels were hit in an organized attack, the results could possibly equal those of 11 September. Unfortunately, detecting and stopping a small launch attacking a larger commercial vessel is almost impossible. It is rapidly becoming apparent that there is a need for real security in the world of shipping.

Terrorists around the world are beginning to explore a terrifying new addition to their arsenal: chemical and biological agents. Unlike nuclear weapons, these agents can be smuggled into a country almost undetected. In some cases they can be manufactured within the country in which they will be used. The delivery system can be a simple crop-spraying aircraft, capable of covering a medium-sized city within minutes. Alternatively, several martyrs could use fire extinguishers to spray the agent from the rooftop of a high-rise building. If well thought out, it would take no more than six terrorists to wipe out a whole city. The threat of bio-terrorism, long ignored and denied, has heightened over the past few years. Both

extremist nations and terrorist organizations have access to the skills required to cultivate some of the most dangerous pathogens and to deploy them as agents in acts of terror.

In 1995 Iraq was discovered to have a large biological weapons programme. It had produced, filled and deployed bombs, rockets and aircraft spray tanks containing bacillus anthracis and the botulinum toxin. In the same year the Japanese cult *Aum Shinryko* released the nerve gas Sarin in the Tokyo subway. Members of this group are also known to have travelled to Zaire in 1992 to obtain samples of the Ebola virus. Yet in the main it is anthrax and smallpox which give the most concern. Anthrax is an organism that is easy to produce in large quantities and extremely stable in its dried form. The effect of aerosolized anthrax on humans is highly lethal. In 1979 an anthrax epidemic broke out in Sverdlovsk in the Soviet Union, the home of a military bio-weapons facility. Some 66 people died, all of whom lived within 4km (2.4 miles) of the facility. Sheep and cattle died along the same wind axis, some as far away as 50km (31 miles).

Bio-Chemical Weapons

Anthrax also raised its head shortly after America suffered the attacks of 11 September. A strange white powder was transported in letters through the mail system. It was later confirmed as weapons-grade anthrax. A small group of people became contaminated and several died. The government took all reasonable precautions to protect both postal workers and the general public, and the problem seems to have diminished. However, anthrax does not pose as much of a problem when compared to other diseases such as smallpox.

Smallpox is caused by a virus spread from person to person. Infected persons have a characteristic fever and rash. After an incubation period of 10 to

12 days, the patient has high fever and pain. Then a rash begins with small papules developing into pustules on day 7 or 8, and finally changing to scabs around day 12. Between 25 and 30 percent of all unvaccinated patients die of the disease. The terrorist potential of aerosolized smallpox is demonstrated by the outbreak in Germany in 1970. A German who had been working in Pakistan became ill with a high fever and diarrhoea. He was admitted to a local hospital on 11 January, where he was isolated due to the fact that medics thought he might have typhoid fever. Three days later a rash appeared and by 16 January he was diagnosed as having smallpox. He was immediately transported to one of Germany's special isolation hospitals, and more than 100,000 persons were swiftly vaccinated. However, the smallpox patient had had a cough.

The cough acted as a large-volume, small-particle aerosol. Consequently, 19 cases of smallpox occurred in the hospital, one of whom died.

Two years later, in February 1972, a similar outbreak went undetected in Yugoslavia. It was four weeks before a correct diagnosis was made, by which time the original carrier was dead and buried. Twenty million people were vaccinated. Some 10,000 people spent several weeks in isolation, while neighbouring countries closed their borders. By the time the situation was under control 175 patients had contracted smallpox and

Below: Power stations, especially nuclear, may have to be ringed with anti-aircraft defences in the future to stop an attack similar to that which destroyed the World Trade Center. But are there the political will and finances for such measures?

35 had died. At the moment we are ill-prepared to deal with a terrorist attack that deploys biological weapons. We need to focus on detection, diagnosis and quick response. This means stockpiling vaccines and drugs, in addition to training and preparing health workers.

Bombs and bio-chemical sprays are not the only weapons in the terrorists' arsenal. Western countries in particular are equally open to an attack on their technological infrastructure. It would be hard to imagine life without computers. In fact, it would be almost impossible for the West to go back to the old days of paper business. The demands of our modern societies are so high that it requires machines to control their functions. Being so reliant on computers makes us vulnerable. Computers support the delivery of goods and services and aid manufacturing, government, banking and finance. What would happen if, for example, the stock exchange computers were put offline for several days or the banks could not issue money to their customers because all the accounts had been wiped out? While both institutions have continuous back-up systems, someone with the right expertise can also find ways of destroying these. All political, military and economic interests depend on information technology, including critical infrastructures such as electric

Below: Cyber warfare is an ever-present possibility in the West. A single person sitting at a computer keyboard can cause damage that runs into millions of dollars.

power, telecommunications and transport. The information technology infrastructure is at risk not only from disruptions and intrusions, but also from serious attacks.

Cyber warfare offers a cloak of obscurity to potential attackers. Additionally, all they need is access to a computer and a telephone line. In March 2001, Japan's Metropolitan Police Department disclosed that a software system it had acquired to track 150 police vehicles, including unmarked cars, had been copied by the *Aum Shinryko* cult. This is the same cult that gassed the Tokyo subway in 1995, killing 12 people and injuring 6000 more. At the time of the discovery, the cult had received classified tracking data on 115 vehicles. Also, the cult had developed software for at least 80 Japanese firms and 10 government agencies. They had worked as subcontractors to other firms, making it almost impossible for the organizations to know who was developing the software. As subcontractors, the cult could have installed "Trojan horses" to launch or facilitate cyber-terrorist attacks at a later date.

Combating the Terrorist Threat

A similar situation arose when the US Government realized that some 150 of its embassies were using software developed and written by citizens of the former Soviet Union. It was quickly removed. Governments and the military have developed software that will detect viruses and hackers entering the system and annul them at source. The computer networks are slowly being hardened with "Firewall" alert protocol and automated response software, but a virtual arms race is set to continue.

The answer to all these possible threats lies in good long-term vigilance and preparation for the worst-case scenario. It's not just nuclear power stations and cities that need to be on their guard:

ships, major sports events and any large congregation of people are all potential targets. We must ask why our intelligence services missed the warning signals for the 11 September attacks. Where were our listening posts, our agents and our monitoring stations? What were the agencies doing wrong? If we are to believe the attacks were carried out by Osama bin Laden, who for the past few years has been hiding in Afghanistan, how did he communicate to the operational unit in America? Telephone and courier traffic would have been fairly obvious, so how come no one spotted either? If, on the other hand, we surmise that our security services were operating as normal, does this indicate that the terrorist's security is getting much better?

The SAS on the Frontline

Using the SAS and other anti-terrorist units, we need to establish international command-and-control organizations, inter-agency communications, intelligent surveillance and reconnaissance teams in terrorist hot-spots. Basically, this means being able to locate, identify and monitor terrorist organizations and predict terrorist activities before they happen. We need to focus on developing and improving the ability to tag and track suspected individuals. Finally, we need men on the ground with the enemy, taking the fight to his backyard. If there is to be any lasting answer it is to eradicate the freedom for terrorists to operate wherever they are based. But we must be careful not to increase the amount of martyrs in the process. There is a balance between violence and peace, which is one of reconciliation. But to attain reconciliation we must first bridge the gap between religions, rich and poor, friend and foe. Looking at the current situation in the Middle East and elsewhere, I think international peace is impossible.

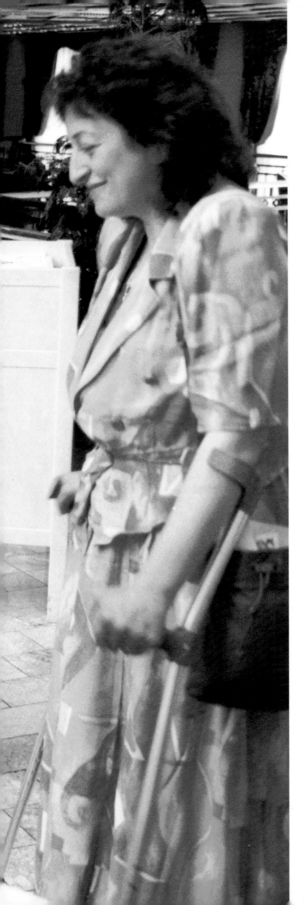

CHAPTER 10

Reflections

In this chapter the author reflects on his meeting with a former enemy and provides an insight into the terrorist's mind. He also looks at three major terrorist groups to show why anti-terrorist units will remain an integral part of governments' arsenals in the future.

Although the purpose of this book is not to define or analyze terrorism, it is worth looking at what makes a terrorist and why terrorist organizations exist. It is an interesting fact that the label "terrorist" is usually associated with "enemy". We must recognize the old adage "one man's terrorist is another man's freedom fighter". For example, you will have read in this book about the exploits of the British anti-terrorist team, yet the SAS has also supplied soldiers to train guerrilla groups around the world. By the same token the US Government, and the Central Intelligence Agency (CIA) in particular, also trained and equipped members of bin Laden's *Al Qaeda* network during the Afghan-Soviet war.

Whenever terrorism is defeated by counter-terrorist units, news of the incident is splashed around the world. Black-clad figures storming the Iranian Embassy in London were seen by millions on prime-time television. The recent war against the Taliban in Afghanistan appeared over in weeks.

Left: Former enemies meet again, though this time not intending to kill each other. The author (left) with the woman he tried to shoot at Mogadishu in 1977: Souhaila Ansari (right).

However, these incidents are rare. This is not the case with the actions of terrorist organizations, most of whom carry out attacks almost on a daily basis. While society may denounce such actions, if we come down to operational results the terrorists are winning. So why is this?

Most governments spend a large part of their budget on military hardware and on anti-terrorist teams who are issued with state-of-the-art equipment. But why do these super fit men who receive specialist training not achieve the same results as the terrorist organizations? The answer is simple: we are on the defensive while they are on the offensive. They act, we react. That is not to say that our anti-terrorist teams are not doing their job,

Below: The young Souhaila Ansari. Born into a prosperous family, her privileged upbringing was interrupted when she saw the sufferings of the Palestinians in Lebanon.

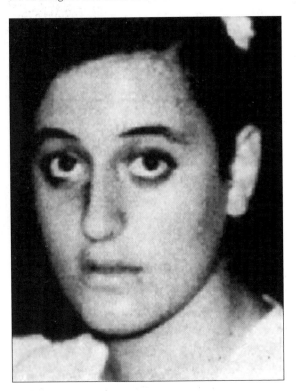

they are. In almost every case where anti-terrorist units have been used they have been successful. Many of these successes have been mentioned in this book, but we would be burying our heads in the sand if we did not make some comparison.

I watch the news most days, and most days I see the carnage caused by terrorism. In Israel a suicide bomber kills himself and 30 other civilians. Two days later Israeli F-16 jets scream over the Gaza Strip and West Bank, blasting rockets into Palestine Liberation Organization (PLO) "security positions" in retribution. Members of *Al Qaeda* hijack aircraft and fly them into heavily populated buildings, killing over 3000 people. Islamic militants in the Philippines kidnap US and German tourists. Terrorism is rarely out of the media. So why do we have terrorists and why do we have terrorist organizations?

The Terrorist

I don't have all the answers, but if I have learnt anything over the past 40 years it's that terrorists are also human beings. It is their cause and the ferocity of their actions which make ordinary members of the public fear them. But trust me, they also have fears. They have homes, mothers and fathers, brothers, sisters, wives and children. If there is a difference between the terrorist and the general public it lies in their belief that their cause is just. Terrorists stem from all walks of life, and range from disillusioned young students to those who see joining terrorist organizations as a way out of their poverty. I have only ever had the opportunity to talk to one such terrorist.

During the Mogadishu hijack in 1977, three of the four Palestinian terrorists were shot dead, one woman survived. She was Souhaila Ansari (she changed her name to Andrawes after her later move to Norway). Back in 1977 I had been one of the soldiers trying to kill her. Eighteen years later I had the opportunity to spend several days talking

Above: A Palestinian refugee camp in Lebanon. The wretched conditions in the camps led to widespread resentment against Israel, and provided a steady stream of terrorist recruits.

with Souhaila in an effort to understand her part in the hijack. This story demonstrates how a person becomes a terrorist.

On 29 January 1995, I stood outside an obscure block of grey flats on the outskirts of Oslo. The day was dull and overcast, lightened only by the thick cover of hard-packed snow which carpeted the land. I stamped my feet in an effort to rejuvenate the circulation, and snuggled deeper inside my overcoat as the wind battled to bring on hypothermia. My visit to Norway was in the interests of military history, but privately I was equally fascinated by the thought of talking to a

former foe. The man with me was Keith Hammet, a Norwegian newspaper reporter who had arranged the meeting. I turned once more to look at the door and read the name on the bottom nameplate: Andrawes.

The last time I had seen this lady she had been called Ansari, Souhaila Ansari, and she was being carried away on a stretcher, her body riddled with bullets. I turned to Keith, who seemed impervious to the cold, and asked: "What the hell am I doing here? This could be a set-up. There could be a Palestinian hit team in there." Even as the words left my lips, old memories and training started flicking through my mind. That's one of the problems about being ex-SAS, it takes years for old habits to disappear. Some of them never do – self-preservation being one of them. I honestly started

Above: The remains of the World Trade Center in New York following the terrorist attacks on 11 September 2001. This event stunned the greatest military power on earth.

Right: "Ground Zero" in New York – the aftermath of the terrorist attacks on the World Trade Center. Ironically, bin Laden had been supported by the CIA in the 1980s.

thinking about diving for cover and looking for escape routes, windows, doors. "Stay alert," I warned myself. Instinctively, I decided to let Keith enter the flat first, at least he would provide me with some form of cover. My morbid thoughts were interrupted by a sharp click as the door opened. Souhaila's lawyer appeared, beckoning Keith and me to enter. I followed both of them into the lobby and up the short flight of stairs, an odd feeling gripping my guts. The flat was on the first floor and

although not large, was warm and pleasant. Several strangers stood as we entered and a young girl, who seemed disinterested in the proceedings, contented herself with getting ready for school. I peered past the assembled bodies until I saw a woman struggling to rise from the settee. I say struggling because she was on crutches. I stared back into the biggest and saddest eyes in the world. Even at that first glance they said "help me". Automatically I went forward to help Souhaila, and the next minute

mixture of sadness and joy, and a weak smile licked at her lips. This is part of the "Stockholm syndrome", where a shared experience for both the victor and the vanquished unites them.

Souhaila was 41, and before the Germans found her she had been living a quiet life as a refugee in Norway. That she took part in the hijack is not in dispute, but she has suffered for it. Her sentence was 20 years in a Mogadishu jail, and although she only served a year before being pardoned, the abusive conditions of a Somali jail equate to several years by Western standards. Additionally, she is held prisoner within her own crippled body, and will be for the rest of her natural life – itself shortened.

The Making of a Terrorist

We started talking. Although I had prepared a list of questions, most relating to technical details about the hijack, it was the warmth of her personal story that enthralled me. Souhaila was born into an upper middle-class Christian family, whose background lay in the Middle East. Her family is cultured, mainly because Christians tend to have small families and can thus afford a better education and schools for their children. She grew up as a Palestinian, and soon became aware of her position in society. She felt different. She was a refugee. When she was still a young girl her parents decided to emigrate to Kuwait, hoping family life would be easier there as Kuwait has an influx of many foreigners who seem to settle quickly in the country.

Success shone on the family and they led a good and prosperous life. Souhaila's life and energy, bottled within her crippled frame, still shines through. It is her eyes you first see, followed by the voice you hear speaking forth the cause of her people, brilliantly recasting their cry for human justice. She claims it was this cry for justice that led her down the path of terrorism. Souhaila was born

we were locked in a warm embrace. For all the world we could have been long-lost friends or lovers, but nothing could be further from the truth.

Until that moment I had always thought of her as the enemy. Confused, I tried to imagine that this was the same woman who 18 years before had fallen badly wounded, cut down in a hail of bullets. I gently eased myself from the embrace and helping her, sat beside her on the settee. Tears were welling from those large brown eyes, moonbeam tears, a in the Lebanon and from the very outset she had wanted to be a nun. She told me: "It was my first dream that I wanted to fulfil. I actually prepared everything, I was all set, my clothes packed, and I was due to travel to Jerusalem in 1967. That was the year the Israelis occupied Jerusalem, and my dream of becoming a nun was shattered when the Israelis destroyed the school." (In the 1967 war, the Israeli Army reached the "Wailing Wall" in Jerusalem, shortly after it had bulldozed many Palestinian homes and buildings.)

The Palestinian Cause

With shattered dreams, Souhaila went to high school in Kuwait, where she achieved very high marks. She said proudly: "I was third out of 20,000 students." This fact disproves the theory that you have to be uneducated to be a terrorist. Her desire to go on to university in Kuwait was crushed, as being a Palestinian she wasn't permitted despite her excellent results from high school. So once again her parents had to send her back to Lebanon to study. It was not an easy decision. First of all she was a beautiful young girl; second, she would be the first one to travel and live away from home. Fortunately, she had both aunts and uncles living in Lebanon, so Souhaila went to live with them, and all the time she was protected. Up until this time she had never seen a refugee camp, but when Souhaila became a third-year student, the war in Lebanon began. For the first time, she met with people from the camps. Souhaila described her feelings: "I felt shame. Here was I living a good and protected life, getting most things I wanted, when close by my people were dying, dying for only one reason – they were Palestinians."

When she first witnessed the camps and the living conditions, a change came over her. "If you had been Palestinian and seen the same sights, you too would have been a terrorist, doing far more

than I ever did. I was not a real soldier like you Barry, I could not kill someone in cold blood like you have done." Fair enough, she had a point. "I saw the massacre, the massacre of 3000 Palestinians, women, children and elderly. All trapped in the camps while soldiers fired artillery into the tents, killing babies and other innocents just because they were Palestinians. Trying to wipe my people off the map. Nobody stopped this slaughter, no one helped, everybody was too busy helping the state of Israel. I was never against Israel, but you British helped give them a home in my land, pushing us out. You forgot about us, closed your eyes to what was happening to our people – nobody came to help. If you have Palestinian blood, if you have a little humanity, then you have to give something for your country, to those poor suffering people, it's your duty."

Black September

Souhaila was referring to the conflict between the Palestinians and the Jordanians. The PLO had constantly raided into Israel from bases in Jordan, and as a result had brought retaliation against Jordan. Matters came to a head when the Popular Front for the Liberation of Palestine (PFLP) hijacked four airliners between 6 and 9 September 1970, forcing three of them to land at an airfield 32km (20 miles) from King Hussein's palace. Hussein capitulated to ensure the safety of the passengers, but once they had been released the planes were blown up. Although none of the passengers were harmed, he turned on the Palestinians. On 16 September he released his Bedouin troops to confront Palestinian forces; at the same time his artillery pounded the refugee camps. Over 3000 were killed and 11,000 wounded. The majority of the people in the camps were civilians. It is from this action that the terrorist group Black September took its name.

Her outburst threw me for a moment. Sitting on the settee Souhaila looked so civilized, unthreatening, while speaking with such compelling eloquence. This was the first time anyone had explained so simply a reason for terrorism; it was so clear and said with such inner feeling. I asked Souhaila how she then became involved. "My family ordered me to return to Kuwait as the situation in the Lebanon was becoming unsafe. But sitting within the safety of my family, eating chocolates and watching television, I became sick – psychologically sick, thinking about my poor people. I tried to run away, but they caught me at the airport and security brought me back. I had wanted to go to Beirut. Then I tried working for the Red Cross helping to raise money for the people in the camps, but soon the campaigning ended and there was no more organized work for women, so I started in a different direction by going to work for a Palestinian magazine. What I didn't know at the time was that one of the editors was a member of the PFLP. That's how I accidentally became involved." The rest I knew, well most of it, but I still wanted to hear Souhaila's version. She has that rare ability to translate her people's longings into something that is understandable.

The Enemy?

Her long battle as a woman to find an identity and equality for the Palestinian people is woven seamlessly into the traumatic 41 years of her life. I was also quickly learning that she had a way with words and a dagger-sharp talent for choosing the right ones; discovering also, that the power of her words was one of the best defences against extradition. Suddenly, here was I, an ex-SAS soldier, listening to a side of the story I had never envisaged. I was perplexed. I thought: "You spend most of your working life learning about death and

destruction, you travel the planet dispensing justice from the barrel of a gun and now you're feeling sympathy for a Palestinian – get real." However, on the flight home many thoughts skimmed across the muddied waters of my reflections. True, she had been a terrorist. She was a Palestinian. They were

Below: A Hamas terrorist in Lebanon. Until the Palestinian situation can be settled to the satisfaction of all parties, such terrorists as these will continue to operate.

the enemy. I decided at that moment to investigate the whole Palestinian-Israeli conflict.

Even though Souhaila's story fascinated me, I still felt she had told me many half-truths. Additionally, what about the innocent, what about the hostages on flight LH181, and what about the murdered pilot Jurgan Schumann. What would their views be on Souhaila?

Terrorist Organizations

As I mentioned above, if I were able to tally a rough head count of all the terrorists killed by anti-terrorist teams and compare it to those killed during terrorist incidents, there is a very strong imbalance in favour of the terrorists. Terrorist organizations exist for one of two reasons: to win or regain territory, or to enforce one political structure over another. Organizations such as the Irish Republican Army (IRA), *Euzkadi ta Askatasuna* (ETA) and *Hamas* (an acronym in Arabic for Islamic Resistance Movement) all seek territorial changes. The IRA wants a united Ireland, ETA wants an independent Basque homeland, and *Hamas* wishes to establish a Palestinian state. These are their sworn statements and their base justification for acts of violence. Because of this, these terrorist groups normally restrict their areas of operation within the territorial bounds of those they oppose.

On the other hand, organizations such as *Al Qaeda* and the Abu Nidal Organisation (ANO) see their cause operating on a much wider front. In the case of the *Al Qaeda* network it is to cause the downfall of all "heretic governments" and to introduce "Shariah" law enforced by Islamic governments. To achieve this, its area of operation is practically anywhere in the world. In all cases, as the fear of terrorism spreads so has the need for governments to counter such actions, at least psychologically, portraying themselves as in control of the chaos. It is not possible to analyze every terrorist organization, so I will restrict myself to a select few.

The IRA has existed since 1919. After the south of Ireland won its independence in 1921 support for the IRA weakened. Infrequent actions continued throughout World War II and during the early 1950s, without any real effect. However the IRA remained intact, albeit in a skeleton form. It re-emerged in its present form in the late 1960s during the civil rights protests. By this time it had transformed itself into the clandestine armed wing of Sinn Fein, a legal political movement dedicated to removing British forces from Northern Ireland and unifying Ireland. Throughout 1970 the troubles exploded into a major battle between the Provisional IRA (PIRA – after a split in the IRA the PIRA became the militant element), various Protestant Loyalist movements and the British Army.

The British Army is Sucked into Sectarianism

At first the Catholic people welcomed the British Army, but they in turn were forced to work alongside the Protestant-dominated police. With the establishment of "no-go" areas in both Londonderry and Belfast, the British Army lost its initial welcome and was seen as supporting Protestants. Shootings and reprisal shootings, bombings and riots took place on a daily basis, and the situation was getting out of control. The British answered this with mass arrests, and by August 1971 had introduced internment without trial for suspected terrorists. This only served to increase the active support for the PIRA, a situation that was not helped by the shooting of 13 Catholic civilians by British paratroopers on 30 January 1972.

"Bloody Sunday", as it became known, was used as a war cry to rally the Catholic people. Direct rule from London was introduced, while in the

Above: *Taliban fighters in Afghanistan. It is somewhat ironic that during the 1980s such fighters were allies of the West against the USSR; now they are among the West's deadliest foes.*

background the British Government tried hard to broker a deal between the Catholic and Protestant factions. When the deal showed no sign of happening, the British Government opted for a hard line against all sides. The army moved in thousands of troops and mounted Operation Motorman, which crushed the no-go areas and re-established authority. This action served to calm the situation somewhat, and the whole shooting match settled down into a permanent British Army commitment.

Towards the end of the 1970s the Province had calmed down considerably, but although the number of attacks declined, those that did take place were particularly brutal. As mentioned in this book, on 27 August 1979 18 members of the Parachute Regiment were killed, while in a separate incident Lord Mountbatten was murdered in the Irish Republic. Four years later, in October 1983, the PIRA made a serious attempt to wipe out the leadership of the Conservative Party when it bombed the conference party hotel in Brighton.

Both the IRA and PIRA work in small cells that consist of about four men. These cells are controlled by the General Council. They also use a series of quartermasters to supply weapons and explosives, together with a host of drivers and couriers. Financial support comes from the local Catholic community and from sympathizers in America. The

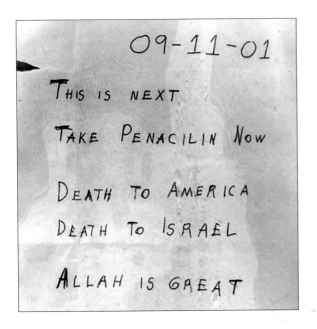

09-11-01

THIS IS NEXT

TAKE PENACILIN NOW

DEATH TO AMERICA

DEATH TO ISRAEL

ALLAH IS GREAT

Above: The close ties between Israel and the United States have resulted in large-scale resentment against the regime in Washington among many Arabs around the world.

IRA is known to have received arms from Libya and explosives training from ETA.

ETA, which translates as "Basque Homeland and Liberty", was founded in 1958. The Basques traditionally inhabit a large area of northern Spain and southwestern France. These people have their own language and culture, which are quite different from those of their neighbours. ETA grew from the nationalist group EKIN, itself formed to counter the inadequate actions of the Basque Nationalist Party during the Franco regime. (Most of the Basque region fought against Franco's Nationalist Party during the Spanish Civil War.) It was at that time the only armed group to emerge in the Spanish state during the Franco era.

Below: In the aftermath of the 11 September 2001 attacks against the US, the country was subjected to anthrax attacks, illustrating the West's vulnerability to biological warfare.

ETA's main aim is the creation of an independent homeland in Spain's Basque region. The region is also its main area of operation, although it has made attacks in France and other parts of Spain. ETA funds come primarily from extorting "Basque revolutionary tax" from the local people, kidnapping ransoms and armed robberies. ETA started its bombing campaign in 1959, concentrating mainly on Bilbao and Santander along the northern coastline. In 1961 ETA made a serious attempt to derail a train carrying civil war veterans, which was travelling to Donostia to celebrate the 25th anniversary of the Spanish Civil War. The attempt failed and the Guardia Civil police responded with brute force. Road blocks were set up across the region and a house-to-house search was made for ETA members or sympathizers. Those who were rounded up were questioned and in some cases tortured. As a result many Basques went into exile in neighbouring France; others stayed to continue ETA's resistance.

ETA Terror

ETA's armed wing – *ETA-Militar* – concentrated its actions mainly against Franco's officials and police, avoiding deaths in the civilian population wherever possible. One of their first major attacks happened in 1973 when the Spanish Prime Minister, Admiral Luis Carrero Blanco, was killed by a massive bomb which ETA had placed in a Madrid street. Admiral Blanco was to be Franco's successor and his death heralded the end of Spanish fascism.

In 1977, a year after Franco's death, the new Spanish democratic government granted substantial autonomy to the country's regions. The Basque region was given its own parliament and was granted control over issues such as education and taxes, while the distinctive Basque language and culture were promoted in schools. Many of those who had been in exile returned. However, this was not far enough for ETA who wanted full independence from Spain. To achieve this it intensified its attacks against the security forces and politicians. Once more its attacks were directed at the military, and in particular the hated Guardia Civil. The latter was eventually changed for a locally recruited security police and the region was given even more autonomy.

Madrid Strikes Back

This sincere approach by the central Spanish Government did much to convince the majority of Basques that independence could be achieved through peaceful means and many started to forsake ETA, turning to the more traditional Basque political parties. The violence abated somewhat. During the socialist government of Felipe Gonzalez, the Anti-Terrorist Liberation Group (GAL) was set up in an attempt to combat ETA's violence. GAL is reportedly responsible for the deaths of 28 suspected ETA members. Their deaths only served to strengthen the resolve of ETA. Yet in July 1997 an estimated six million Spanish people took to the streets to condemn ETA violence, following the brutal kidnapping and murder of a young Basque politician.

The Spanish Government came down hard on all ETA organizations, with policies which included imprisonment for all members of its political arm. There has always been a strong link between ETA and the IRA. Since the recent peace agreement in Northern Ireland, ETA has announced its first ceasefire since its inception. The Spanish Government was wary of such a declaration and dismissed the ceasefire. Although there was a major decline in ETA attacks , it did re-stock its armoury by raiding arms and munitions depots.

ETA continues to carry out terrorist attacks in a campaign that has caused more than 1000 deaths. In 1995 it planned to kill King Juan Carlos while he was on holiday in Majorca, but the plan was discovered. That same year it made an assassination attempt on Jose Maria Aznar, the present Spanish prime minister. The bomb that had been placed in his car was discovered. Three years later a similar car bomb planted by ETA killed Popular Party councillor Manuel Zamarreno.

Hamas

Hamas is a radical Islamic organization created in late 1987 as an expansion of the Palestinian branch of the Muslim Brotherhood. Hamas, which to many followers translates as "courage" or "bravery", is the Arabic short form for Harakat al-Muqawamah al-Islamiyya, this translating as "Islamic Resistance Movement". The group uses both political and aggressive means, including terrorism, to pursue the goal of establishing an Islamic Palestinian state to replace Israel. Hamas is particularly good at using the mosques when it comes to recruiting and fundraising, much of which comes from the Gaza Strip where Hamas is strongest, although it does have influence in the West Bank. Hamas receives funding from individuals in Saudi Arabia and other moderate Arab states. Likewise, many wealthy expatriates living in France, Great Britain and North America also support the organization. There are very few details relating to the hard-core elements of Hamas, but it boasts tens of thousands of supporters and sympathizers.

Since 1991 Hamas has become the primary architect of terrorist activity throughout the Palestinian territories as well as inside Israel, making it the strongest opposition group to the Middle East peace process.

Its military strength is gained through the use of Izz al-Din al-Qassam squads (suicide bombers), who conduct large-scale suicide bombings against Israeli civilians and military targets. On 1 June 2001, a Hamas suicide bomber detonated an explosive device amid a group of youngsters outside the Dolphinarium nightclub. Hundreds of young Israelis, including many Israeli Arabs, gather around the area's beachfront nightclubs and discotheques every Friday night. The club is particularly fashionable with the children of new immigrants from the former Soviet Union. The Palestinian concealed the bomb around his waist and waited until around 23:00 hours, when the promenade was full of young people. The blast killed 20 people and injured more than 120. At 02:00 hours on 9 August 2001, another Hamas suicide bomber detonated a bomb in a pizza restaurant near the centre of Jerusalem. The pizzeria is located at one of the busiest street corners in the city and is a favourite with the younger generation. The blast killed 15 people and wounded more than 90 others. Many of the victims were young families. Five of the dead were all from the same family, including the parents and three children aged 14, 4 and 2. Two other daughters, aged 8 and 7, were severely wounded. In total some six children were among the dead.

Al Qaeda

There are few people in the world who have not now heard the name Osama bin Laden or the Al Qaeda network. Bin Laden was a veteran of the Afghan war against the former Soviet Union. He arrived in Afghanistan in 1979, the same year that Soviet troops invaded. Recognizing the weakness of the Afghan resistance, he organized a recruitment drive through the office Maktab al-Khidamat (MAK). This office called up Muslim followers from

Saudi Arabia, Algeria, Egypt, Pakistan and the Sudan, while many others came from America and Great Britain. At the time the US also wanted the Soviets out of Afghanistan, and a major CIA operation was put in place to aid such promising men as Osama bin Laden. It is estimated that some $500 million a year was pumped into training and arming the *Mujahedin* factions.

Bin Laden's Army

Towards the end of the Soviet-Afghan war, bin Laden had at least 10,000 soldiers under his command, all trained in guerrilla warfare and equipped with American weaponry. While some of these fighters returned to their mother country and continued a peaceful life, others had become indoctrinated by Islamic fundamentalism and began setting up their own organizations, almost all loyal to bin Laden. Some time later ex-*Mujahedin* fighters started to appear in Somalia, Kosovo and Chechnya. Around this time bin Laden split with MAK co-founder Abdallah Azzam and formed *Al Qaeda*. A year later Azzam was killed when a bomb was placed under his car. With the Afghan war ended Osama bin Laden departed to his native Saudi Arabia. After his brief attempt at insurrection, however, the Saudi Government expelled him to Sudan. Here he set up in business constructing airports, roads and several farms. Much of the work he gave to veterans of the Afghan war.

After some American pressure on the Sudanese Government, bin Laden moved once more to Afghanistan. In 1988 he established a multi-national support group to aid the activities of Islamic militants worldwide. Their basic strategy is to overthrow "heretic governments" and the establishment of Islamic governments based on the rule of strict "Shariah" Islamic law. It is known that bin Laden was connected to the bombing of the United States embassies in Dar es Salaam, Tanzania, and Nairobi, Kenya, in which a total of 200 people died. However, even these pale in comparison to the attacks on the World Trade Center's twin towers in New York, an atrocity which bin Laden describes on video as being a "legitimate target". Until the recent war on terrorism bin Laden was based in Afghanistan, from where he controlled his worldwide network. Since the American attack on the country, and at the time of writing, he has disappeared.

Bin Laden may have disappeared, but terrorism is still very much with us. Anti-terrorist units will thus be fully employed for the foreseeable future.

Below: *Osama bin Laden, at present one of the world's most wanted terrorists. His Al Qaeda network has supporters all over the world ready to strike at democratic nations.*

Index

Italic page numbers refer to illustrations